Early Childrearing by Young Mothers:

A Research Study

EARLY CHILDREARING BY YOUNG MOTHERS:
A RESEARCH STUDY

Lucille J. Grow

Child Welfare League of America, Inc.
67 Irving Place, New York, NY 10003

This research was supported through grant OCD-CB-456, Children's Bureau, Office of Child Development, U.S. Department of Health, Education and Welfare.

CHILD WELFARE LEAGUE OF AMERICA

67 Irving Place, New York, New York 10003

Library of Congress Catalog Card Number: 79-53504

ISBN: 0-87868-138-8

Current printing (last digit)
10 9 8 7 6 5 4 3 2

PRINTED IN THE UNITED STATES OF AMERICA

Dedicated to Welles Carter Westbrook. Welles was born on August 14, 1973, and died on October 5, 1977.   His mother, Veronika, participated in the pretest of the instruments used in this study.

CONTENTS

ACKNOWLEDGMENTS

This study was made possible through grant #OCD-CB-456 from the Office of Child Development. During most of the study, Mrs. Cecelia Sudia was Project Officer for administration of the grant. Her support, her comments and suggestions were invaluable.

Barbara Kreger, who early in the study replaced Barbara Tint as research assistant, had major responsibility for the "bookkeeping," coding, and correspondence with the interviewers. Both she and the project director were novices with computers and especially with the SPSS system. By the time the study terminated Ms. Kreger was an expert. Her patience, attention to detail and cooperation are appreciated.

Many persons in Wisconsin, the site of the project population, contributed to the study. The project could not have been launched without the initial and ongoing assistance of three Milwaukee agencies--Catholic Social Services, Children's Service Society of Wisconsin, and Wisconsin Lutheran Child and Family Service--and the Wisconsin State Department of Health and Social Services.

Special thanks are due to Patricia Fetterley, health consultant at Catholic Social Services. That agency volunteered Ms. Fetterley's services as chauffeur to the project director during the hospital recruitment phase. Ms. Fetterley provided more than chauffeur service; it was her enthusiasm for the study and her familiarity with hospital personnel that contributed to enlistment of the cooperation of Milwaukee hospitals.

The following hospitals participated in the study: Columbia, Doctor's, Lutheran, Milwaukee County General, Mt. Sinai Medical Center, Northwest General, St. Anthony,

St. Francis, St. Joseph's, St. Luke's, St. Mary's, St. Michael, Salvation Army Booth Memorial, Trinity Memorial and West Allis Memorial. In addition, Rosalie Manor, a maternity residence adjacent to Milwaukee County, participated.

Patricia Costello was employed as the local coordinator. Her familiarity with persons on the local scene was helpful, particularly during the recruitment stage of study subjects.

An immeasurable debt of gratitude is owed the interviewers. Their energy, determination and enthusiasm account for the low rate of attrition during the 3-year interviewing period. Four interviewers conducted interviews at all three time periods--Nancy Anderson, Susan Brophy, Judy Konkol and Bonnie Pomo. Nancy Smith participated in the Time 1 interviews. When she moved to another state, she was replaced by Mary Ellen Chabot and Patricia Neuenfeldt, who interviewed at both Times 2 and 3.

Appreciation is also owed to Dr. Deborah Shapiro, former Director of Research at CWLA, for her suggestions and support. Carl Schoenberg and Edward Zusi provided editorial support and advice, and Anne Moore did all the typing.

Many others also contributed to this study. Most important are the study participants, who gave of their time and provided the essential data.

PREFACE

In the early 1970s the increase in births to single white women raised many questions for society, and particularly for professionals in the child welfare field.   Studies suggested a trend for these young mothers to resort to plans other than adoption, with undetermined consequences both for the mother and the child.   Until the early 1970s little reliable information was available about the young white unmarried parent, because in the past research had focused on black unmarried women and their children.

This research project, financed by the Office of Child Development, Department of Health, Education and Welfare, was therefore undertaken to study a sample of young white mothers and their children over a 3-year period. Both unmarried and married mothers were included in the sample, to provide a basis of comparison. The findings are based upon a study of a group of white primiparas under 25, over half of whom were Roman Catholic and all of whom came from one county in a Midwest state. Although these limiting factors should be considered in making generalizations applicable to the population at large, the study's results have important implications for all agencies providing child welfare services.

If agencies are to meet the needs of young white parents and their infants, programs should provide comprehensive services for the parent who keeps her child. Although adoption was initially considered by 41% of the unmarried mothers in this study, only 3% of the children were permanently surrendered within the first year of life. Furthermore, at the end of the 3-year period relatively few of the children had experienced a disruption in the continuity of care, and with rare exceptions all the children were still cared for by their biological mothers.

In their programming, social agencies should take cognizance of the importance of the availability of concrete community supportive services, including day care, information on child care, and opportunities for the mothers to share their experiences and concerns with other young mothers. Agencies should take the initiative in providing such services themselves and in promoting use of existing community resources.

Social agencies not only should have comprehensive programs readily available, but must find ways to inform young parents about these services. An aggressive reaching out to young mothers and fathers and the extended family as well is imperative if social agencies are to be responsive to the concerns expressed in this study.

It behooves the field of child welfare to face up to the current reality. Changes in program emphasis are long overdue. Today the major need of young parents, married and unmarried, and their infants is comprehensive communitywide services accessible to all.

Katherine Daly, Director
Florence Crittenton Division, CWLA

Early Childrearing by Young Mothers:

A Research Study

CHAPTER 1
INTRODUCTION

The idea for this study had been fermenting for several years prior to the development of the study proposal and design. During the mid-1960s social agencies in various parts of the country began reporting two related trends: 1) despite an increase in white out-of-wedlock births, fewer white unwed mothers were using maternity residences and other social agency services; 2) more white mothers who did seek such services were keeping their babies.

Some considered these early reports, particularly relative to the shift away from adoption planning, as based on general impressions, as idiosyncratic to particular agencies and not generalizable to the child welfare field as a whole. In many instances the agencies were not able to substantiate their reports with "hard facts"; yet it seemed likely that agencies reporting such experiences were more acutely sensitized either by locale or agency structure to the possibility that changes from the traditional white single-parent adoption formula might be in the offing.

The possibility that the single, white pregnant woman might begin to avail herself of options other than the customary secrecy of the maternity residence-adoption route seemed obvious. Unmarried couples had begun living together without evoking the same degree of social opprobrium met in the past. Many couples became parents by accident or choice, and elected to begin childrearing without the formality of a marriage contract. The role of the traditional nuclear family as nurturer and educator was challenged.

The women's movement, organized in the early 1960s, is a force for social change that has consequences not only in the marketplace but in the home. The movement

1

encouraged women to reevaluate their status in society, to bear witness to their own needs for self-realization and fulfillment and to challenge their assigned role with regard to childrearing. There has been an increased awareness of female sexuality and a growing demand to discard the stereotype of female passivity. There has been increasing acceptance of women's right to self-determination with regard to abortion; it has become more acceptable for a woman to choose to have a child without acquiring a husband.

Women's increased sexual awareness and technological advances in birth control undoubtedly contributed to removal of a taboo on discussions of sex. Attitudes have changed so that sex and its consequences are no longer regarded solely as a moral issue. The proliferation of sex education courses even at the elementary school level, the successful drive to provide continued education for the pregnant teen-ager either in special classes or regular school, have contributed to greater understanding and acceptance of those who purposefully or, more usually accidentally, become pregnant out of wedlock.

In the past, pregnancy out of wedlock met with strong social disapproval. If the expectant mother were white, she was likely either to enter into a hasty marriage or to surrender her child for adoption soon after birth. If she did not marry, her pregnancy usually was cloaked in secrecy. With the partial removal of the moral stigma and the growing awareness that pregnancy out of wedlock is not restricted to any social class, racial group or pathological segment of society, the white unwed mother less often has to make a secret of pregnancy, and has options other than adoption.

Evidence of the shift away from adoption as the favored option for white unwed mothers can be seen in the following data. In 1966 Herzog estimated that about 70% of white children born out of wedlock were surrendered for adoption (1). Later natality statistics reveal that between 1968 and 1974 there was about a 9% increase in the estimated number of white out-of-wedlock live births (2). During this period, a 49% decrease in adoptions by

2

unrelated petitioners of children born out of wedlock was reported by the 20 states that were able to provide reasonably complete data (3).

These trends strongly attest to a shift in the solution to out-of-wedlock pregnancy on the part of the white population. Although many white women may be opting for abortion, a sizable number have chosen not only to carry their babies to term, but resort to plans other than adoption.

RELATED RESEARCH

During the last 20 years there has been an increase in both the rate and number of all out-of-wedlock births. Although 1970 and 1971 saw a slight decrease in such births, from 1972 on the number of white out-of-wedlock births has continued to rise. The numerous studies conducted during this period, especially during the 1960s, no doubt reflect concern about this increase and the consequence of out-of-wedlock pregnancy for both mother and child.

A. Medical and Physical Consequences Associated With Births Out of Wedlock

Many writers have stated that children born out of wedlock suffer handicaps with respect to their physical development and subsequent health (4) and that ". . . . .mortality rates and other health and social indices show out of wedlock infants and their mothers to be in greater need of health and social services" (5). Specialized health services have been developed for unwed mothers and their children because they are believed to "fare considerably less well than in-wedlock mothers and children . . . in terms of morbidity and mortality" (6). The limited data available on this subject do not, however, uniformly support this hypothesis. In addition, the medical data on the sequelae of out-of-wedlock births are further limited in that they rarely refer to consequences occurring after the first year of life.

3

Some studies have attempted to document that children of unmarried mothers have a greater risk of death and disease, but most have limited significance because of their failure to control for such variables as maternal age, parity, socioeconomic status and prenatal care, all important factors in the etiology of infant immaturity and infant loss (7, 8). Pakter et al., (9) who analyzed birth certificates of all children born in New York City in 1955-1959, found that there was a higher incidence of premature births among infants born to both white and nonwhite mothers who were not married. However, in this New York City study, as well as others that linked out-of-wedlock births to physical handicaps, there were more women in the unmarried group who were primiparas under age 20 who had had little or no prenatal care, than in the married control group.

On the other hand, Parmelee reported data that suggest that wedlock status is not an important factor in birth outcome (10). In studying birth weight data of children born to women in a Los Angeles maternity residence for unmarried mothers, he found no significant differences in the immaturity rates by marital status of the mother, noting that the percentage of immature births among unmarried mothers in his study was 7.7%, a percentage almost identical with all births in 1963. Bruns and Cooper, (11) who conducted an extensive investigation into the factors influencing immaturity in a Colorado maternity hospital, did not present data directly related to this subject, but did suggest in their concluding comments that out-of-wedlock status "does not appear to predispose to prematurity."

One study attempted to isolate the effect of unwed motherhood on immaturity and perinatal mortality by comparing the experiences of 2064 Finnish unmarried mothers with a control group of married women with whom they were individually matched on the basis of maternal age, parity and social status (12). No differences were noted in the extent of perinatal mortality in the wed and unwed groups. A significant difference in the rate of immaturity of babies of wed and unwed mothers disappeared when an additional control on amount of prenatal care was introduced. These data, along with the data of several of the authors cited earlier, suggest that unmarried motherhood per se does not influence pregnancy outcome, but rather that out-of-wedlock births are associated with demographic and social variables--particularly youthful motherhood, first births, low income and failure to seek medical care during pregnancy--that lead to higher frequency of infant morbidity and mortality.

B. Economic, Social and Emotional Consequences Associated With Births Out of Wedlock

Children born out of wedlock are believed to experience economic disadvantage, since they are assumed to be more likely than children born in wedlock to be reared in female-headed households, and a high proportion of female-headed households have incomes below the poverty level. The proportion of households with female heads below the poverty level was 36% in 1974, compared with 5% of households with male heads (13).

Comparative studies of the characteristics of unmarried mothers who keep and those who surrender their babies further suggest that the former are less advantaged with respect to education and familial supports.

Meyer and his colleagues studied a sample of unwed mothers with a view to predicting the decisions of unmarried mothers about keeping or surrendering the babies (14). Of the 105 white, never-married mothers known to two maternity residences in 1954, Vincent compared those who relinquished their babies with those who kept them (15). This writer examined the characteristics of a sample of the women included in a national data collection project sponsored by three national agencies that serve unmarried mothers (16). Festinger studied the characteristics of unwed mothers known to Louise Wise Services in 1967-1968 who decided to keep or surrender their babies (17). In these studies older age, lower education, employment rather than school attendance, and a nonintact parental home have tended to be associated with decisions to keep.

Although there have been several followup studies of mothers who keep their babies, relatively little recent information is available on white, unmarried mothers who do so. Furthermore, the different studies are at variance in findings, as well as in the age, parity and other characteristics of the samples. In 1952 Levy followed up 54 women served by Inwood House, a maternity residence, 7 years earlier (18). Thirty-nine of these women were white. Ten of the 18 mothers who had planned to keep their babies still had them in their care, but eight had placed the children in adoption, foster care or with relatives. Compared with those who surrendered their children for adoption, fewer of the women who kept their babies later married, and more of them had other out-of-wedlock children. In 1962, Bowerman et al. studied nearly 1000 North Carolina unwed mothers, predominantly from "blue collar" homes (19). Although the white child was more likely to be adopted than the nonwhite, almost half of the white unwed mothers were still single and had their children with them 6 months to 30 months after their birth. A fourth of the white women had married, but usually someone other than the reputed father.

Reed reported on a followup study in the early 1960s of 118 women, identified through health or welfare agencies, who had kept their babies (20). About three-fourths of the mothers were white. The children were between 9 months and 5 years of age at the time of followup. Reed stressed the seriously disadvantaged status of many of the mothers with respect to housing and financial situation, but reported that 101 of the mothers said they would make the decision to keep if they had it to do again. Wright interviewed 80 of a sample of 290 unwed mothers who had given birth 3 to 4 years earlier and who had been known to social agencies (21). Less than 60% were white. Wright reported satisfactory outcomes for most of these mothers and their children, not only with respect to their environmental and physical situation, but their psychological and social adjustment. Olander re-

6

ported a followup about 3 months after delivery, of 103 unmarried mothers who had planned to take their babies home (22). She found this group, of whom 62% were nonwhite, in precarious economic situations, living in poor and crowded housing, lonely and isolated from social contacts, and needing service in many areas.

In 1962 Sauber and Rubenstein identified 364 women who had their first births in a New York City hospital and who were not considering surrender (23). The women, most of them nonwhite and of low economic background, were interviewed in the hospital, again 18 months later, and again when the child was about 6 years old. A wealth of information on these women is included in the reports. Of particular pertinence is the fact that all but 30 (14%) of the mothers interviewed in the final followup had their children with them; only two children had been adopted and two were in the care of social agencies. The women were found to have many problems common to families who live in poverty, and over half were judged to have personal and social adjustment problems, but few expressed regret at their decision to keep the child.

A British publication reports a followup in 1965 of out-of-wedlock births in 1958 with comparative data for in-wedlock births in the same period (24). On most of the variables presented, the out-of-wedlock births are subdivided into "the adopted sample" of 160 children and "the out-of-wedlock sample" that includes the remaining 504 children born out of wedlock on whom followup information was obtained. Although no differences were found in social class background and upbringing between mothers having an in-wedlock or out-of-wedlock birth, at followup the families of the out-of-wedlock sample showed marked downward social mobility. The home environment of the out-of-wedlock sample was much more unfavorable than that of the adopted sample or the children born in-wedlock, as indicated by degree of overcrowding, lack of household amenities and the use of substitute care on a day or residential basis. One in nine of the children in this sample, as compared with one in 50 in the whole cohort, had had one or more separation experiences, with the first separation frequently occurring before the age of 18 months. With regard to the physical development of the children themselves, there were no marked differences between the children born out of wedlock and those born in wedlock. On tests of "abilities and attainments," however, the sample of children born out of wedlock scored significantly lower than the others, and the incidence of maladaptive behavior in school was much higher. This is the most comprehensive study that has come to our attention, but it concerns births in England almost 20 years ago.

A more recent study is a followup of over 300 primiparous adolescent mothers who had registered at a Baltimore prenatal clinic between 1966 and 1968 (25). Three-fourths of these women had been single at the time of their baby's birth and nine-tenths of the mothers were black. When these mothers were reinterviewed in 1972, the vast majority still had their children living with them and most of the mothers reported having made a successful adjustment to parenthood. Furstenberg also attempted to measure the cognitive development and social maturity of those children who were 3½ years of age or older. Although the cognitive performance of the children, as measured by a modified and shortened version of the Preschool Inventory, was lower than those of three comparison groups of children attending preschool, the children's scores indicated above-average preschool readiness, as compared with the scores of the Head Start children on whom the test had been standardized. The test for social maturity included four interpersonal indices, and Furstenberg reported no marked difference between the study children and the other groups on any of these measures. However, he did find an association between socioeconomic status and cognitive development, as well as an indication that at least on two measures of social development, economic disadvantage contributed to maladjustment.

STUDY OBJECTIVE

The unwed mother and her child have been described as medical and social high risk groups. It has been

8

hypothesized that children born out of wedlock are more likely than children born in wedlock to be deprived of a two-parent family and, as a result, suffer with regard to their physical, mental and emotional development (26). Although it is assumed that a substantial portion of the disadvantage to the child born out of wedlock is related to the greater probability of being reared in a one-parent family, little formal research has been conducted to evaluate the effect of being born out of wedlock and reared, at least initially, in a single-parent environment. Most of the research has been concerned with black unmarried women and their children; how generalizable these findings are to white families is not known. This study was restricted to young white mothers.

In addition, the circumstances of the young single women who keep their babies vary widely. Some marry soon after their baby's birth. Others live with the child's father or with another man in a conjugal relationship that may be transitory or reasonably permanent. Some live in their parents' home, where relatives are available to assist in child care. Some live alone, with little family support, as they attempt to cope with their own needs and those of the child. What problems these young mothers encounter in the care of their children and how the source, nature and continuity of this care compare with those of children of young mothers who were legally married at the time of their baby's birth is a matter of serious interest to students of family life and child development.

Concern has been expressed by child welfare agencies that well intended childrearing plans break down, with the result that some young unmarried mothers neglect their children and others seek substitute care for them when the children have reached an age at which separation is more traumatic than in early infancy and, also, when appropriate care for the child is more difficult to obtain. Of specific interest to child welfare service agencies are the kinds of living arrangement and familial and extra-familial support that predict the single mother's ability to cope adequately with her parental responsibilities; the community supportive services that would enhance the parental care; and the circumstances under which successful childrearing is so

9

unlikely that the single girl in such circumstances should be helped to consider alternative plans.

We have been emphasizing the problems of the young single mother and her child, for it was the reported increase in the number and proportion of young unmarried mothers who keep their children that stimulated development of this study. Yet some of the untoward consequences ascribed to out-of-wedlock births may well be consequences of the mother's age, parity and socioeconomic status rather than of her marital status. Furthermore, as suggested earlier, the family structure into which the single woman brings her child is not uniform. Many of these women subsequently marry (27). Likewise, many pregnant young women marry to avoid giving birth out of wedlock. Since early marriages show a relatively high divorce rate, (28) the child born to the young married woman is not guaranteed a stable family structure. The circumstances of the young married woman and her first child are therefore of interest not only as a basis of comparison with those of the unmarried mother and her child, but because little is known about them and about the support services needed by the young married mother to facilitate her childrearing.

This study is therefore addressed to the following questions:

1) What are significant social and behavioral characteristics, experiences and attitudes of young white primiparous mothers?

2) What are the major differences in social and behavioral characteristics, experiences and attitudes of women who were married and those who were unmarried at the time their baby was born?

3) Do early differences by marital status persist or do they disappear in time?

4) Are social characteristics of the mother--such as age, marital status, education, childhood experiences, parental socioeconomic status, economic level at the outset of childrearing--predictive of her sense of well-being and ease with which she assumes responsibility for her child care role?

10

5) Which, if any, social characteristics are predictive of the well-being of her child at age 3?

6) What effect do other aspects such as attitudinal components, physical and emotional health, familial and community supports, and the mother's childrearing practices have on outcome for mother and child?

Chapter 2 presents the general design of the study. Chapters 3 through 7 describe data obtained in interviews with the mothers at three points in time, as well as specifying significant differences found between mothers married at the time of their baby's birth and those who were unmarried. Chapter 8 is devoted to the findings related to questions 4 through 6.

REFERENCES

1. Herzog, Elizabeth. "The Chronic Revolution: Births Out of Wedlock," Clinical Pediatrics, 5 (1966), 132.

2. National Center for Health Statistics. Monthly Vital Statistics Report, Advance Report. Final Natality Statistics, 1968 and 1974.

3. United States Department of Health, Education and Welfare, Social and Rehabilitation Service, National Center for Social Statistics. Adoptions in 1968 and Adoptions in 1974.

4. National Center for Health Statistics. Trends in Illegitimacy in the United States, 1940-1965, Series 21, #5, 1968.

5. Teele, J., and Schmidt, W. "Illegitimacy and Race: National and Local Trends," Milbank Memorial Fund Quarterly, 48 (1970), 127.

6. Anderson, U.R., et al. "The Medical, Social and Educational Implications of the Increase in Out-of-Wedlock Births," American Journal of Public Health, 56 (1966), 1866.

7. Parmelee, A. "Prematurity and Illegitimacy," American Journal of Obstetrics and Gynecology, 100 (1968), 7.

8. Bruns, P., and Cooper, W. "Basic Factors Influencing Premature Birth," Clinical Obstetrics and Gynecology, 4 (1961), 341.

9. Pakter, J., et al., "Out-of-Wedlock Births in New York City, Medical Aspects," American Journal of Public Health, 51 (1961), 846.

10. Parmelee, op. cit.

11. Bruns and Cooper, op. cit.

12. Paavola, A. "The Illegitimacy Rate and Factors Influencing Pregnancy and Delivery of Unmarried Mothers," Acta Obstetrica et Gynecologica, Scandinavia, 47 (1968), 7.

13. United States Department of Commerce, Bureau of the Census. Characteristics of the Population Below Poverty Level, 1974, Series P-60, # 102.

14. Meyer, Henry J., et al. "The Decision by Unmarried Mothers to Keep or Surrender Their Babies," Social Work, 1 (1956), 103-109.

15. Vincent, Clark. Unmarried Mothers. New York: Free Press of Glencoe, (1961), 185-201.

16. Grow, Lucille J. "The Unwed Mother Who Keeps Her Child," in The Double Jeopardy--The Triple Crisis: Illegitimacy Today. New York: National Council on Illegitimacy, 1969, 115-125.

17. Festinger, Trudy Bradley. "Unwed Mothers and Their Decisions to Keep or Surrender Their Children," Child Welfare, 50 (1971), 253-263.

12

18. Levy, Dorothy. "A Followup Study of Unmarried Mothers," Social Casework, 36 (1955), 27-33.

19. Herzog, Elizabeth. "Unmarried Motherhood: Personal and Social Consequences," Welfare in Review, 2 (August 1964), 20-22.

20. Reed, Ellery F. "Unmarried Mothers Who Kept Their Babies," Children, 12 (1965), 118-119.

21. Wright, Helen R., 80 Unwed Mother Who Kept Their Babies. Sacramento: California Department of Social Welfare, Children's Home Society of California, Los Angeles County Bureau of Adoptions, May 1965.

22. Olander, Jeanne. The Single Parent and Her Baby: Implications for Community Action. San Francisco: The Single Parent Project, 1967.

23. Sauber, Mignon, and Rubenstein, Elaine. Experiences of the Unwed Mother as a Parent. New York: Community Council of Greater New York, 1965; also, Sauber, Mignon, and Corrigan, Eileen M. The Six-Year Experience of Unwed Mothers as Parents. New York: Community Council of Greater New York, 1970.

24. Crellin, Eileen; Pringle, Kellmer M.L.; and West, Patrick. Born Illegitimate: Social and Educational Implications. London: National Foundation for Educational Research in England and Wales, 1971.

25. Furstenberg, Frank F., Jr. Unplanned Parenthood: The Social Consequences of Teen-age Childbearing. New York: Free Press, 1976.

26. Whelan, E.M. "Estimates of the Ultimate Family Status of Children Born Out-of-Wedlock," Journal of Marriage and the Family, (November, 1972).

27. Ibid.

28. United States Department of Commerce, Bureau of the Census. <u>Current Population series</u>, P-20, # 223, "Social and Economic Variations in Marriage, Divorce and Remarriage," 1971.

CHAPTER 2
GENERAL DESIGN OF THE STUDY

GENERAL DESIGN AND LOCALE

The design of the study may be described as diagnostic-descriptive, in Kahn's terminology (1). The general plan was to identify at time of delivery a cohort of white, unmarried primiparas under age 25 who planned to keep their babies and a comparison group of white, married primiparas under age 25, and to follow up both groups for 3 years. These women were to be interviewed within a month of discharge from the hospital and interviewed again when their child was 18 months old and 36 months old. To minimize attrition and maintain cooperation, telephone contacts with the mothers were to be made every 6 months between the first and third interviews. Three years were believed to be the minimum period of followup that would permit assessment of the child's well-being and the continuity of care. By that time, the single woman's plans to keep her child would have had a chance to be tested, and the married woman would have passed a stage when many young marriages founder.

Milwaukee County, Wisconsin, was selected as the site of the research for reasons of size (population 717,000), racial composition (under 16% nonwhite), social climate (relatively conservative), the interest of the Wisconsin Department of Health and Social Services, and the availability of several member agencies of the Child Welfare League of America to facilitate operations.

Originally, the plan was to obtain the study population solely through the 15 hospitals in Milwaukee County that reported 100 or more deliveries annually, and through one maternity residence adjacent to Milwaukee County.

Since the hospitals could not release the names of their patients without their consent, a form was devised that was distributed by hospital personnel to each potentially eligible mother. The form described the purpose of the study and requested the mother's signature, address and phone number so that an interviewer might tell her more about the study. The mother could then decide whether she wished to participate.

Each hospital appointed one or more staff members responsible for seeing that primiparous, white, married and unmarried mothers under 25 years of age received this form. The persons delegated this responsibility included nurses, social service staff and health coordinators.

The initial plan was to have a sample consisting of an equal number of married and unmarried women living within a 100-mile radius of Milwaukee, who delivered in one of the participating hospitals or else in the maternity residence. Since it was anticipated that the number of married women would far exceed the number of unmarried women, a random sample of married women was to be selected each week, equal to the number of unmarried women who agreed to participate.

SELECTION OF STUDY SUBJECTS AND FINAL STUDY POPULATION

Recruitment of study subjects through the hospitals and maternity residence commenced on November 1, 1973, and was to continue through April 1974. It soon was clear that although consents were received from a substantial number of married women and from a much smaller number of unmarried women, neither group represented the eligible population. Busy hospital personnel were not always able to contact potentially eligible mothers, particularly those women whose confinement occurred over a weekend or who were in hospital for only a few days. Since so few consents from unmarried women were received, the support of the Milwaukee social agencies and the State Department of Health and Social Services was enlisted to achieve access to the eligible unmarried women who were not being contacted while in the hospitals. The recruitment period for unmarried mothers was extended 2 months, although most of these unmarried women had delivered during the original 6-month planned recruitment phase. Because there was no way of estimating the number of unmarried women who would agree to participate, during the second half of the hospital recruitment period random sampling of married mothers was discontinued and all married women who agreed to participate during the last 3 months were included in the study.

During the period in which potential study subjects were recruited, hospital consent forms were received from 344 eligible married women, and 287 of these women were selected as potential study subjects. We received consent forms from or else received notification through the State Department of the existence of 312 eligible unwed women.

As can be seen from Table 2-1, completed interviews were obtained from three-fourths of the potential study subjects. Although they agreed to have the interviewer contact them, 22 married women subsequently refused to participate, usually because their husbands opposed the study, or they were too busy, or were not interested. An additional three married women could not be located, and health problems of one mother made an interview inappropriate.

Table 2-1
Potential Study Population Identified at Time 1 (First Interview)

	Married		Unmarried		Total	
	No.	%	No.	%	No.	%
Completed interviews	261	91	187	60	448	75
Refusals	22	8	56	18	78	13
Unable to locate	3	1	69	22	72	12
Mother seriously ill	1	*	–	–	1	*
Total	287	100	312	100	599	100

* Less than 1%

Failure to locate the potential respondent was, not surprisingly, the major reason for loss among the unmarried women. The names and addresses of most of these women were furnished by the State Department, and it is possible that many gave false addresses. Among the refusals, many women expressed a lack of interest or repeatedly failed to keep appointments. In some instances the mother was hostile toward the interviewer; in several instances the mother was reluctant to participate because of a desire to protect the baby's father. (The final sample is indicated in the section on Interviews and Attrition.)

DATA COLLECTION INSTRUMENTS

The major data collection instruments were interview schedules, containing both open-ended and closed-response questions, that explored various aspects of the lives of the mothers, and to a lesser extent of their children. With rare exception the interviews were conducted in the mothers' homes and usually took from 2 to 2½ hours. The first interview, usually in the month following the mother's discharge from hospital, inquired into her background and parental socioeconomic status, her motivation for parenthood, prenatal and postnatal care of mother and baby, her current situation and her attitude toward and plans for care of her child.

The second interview, administered when the child was about 1½ years of age, sought information on the mother's and child's current living situation, the child's health and development, the relationship of mother and child to the child's father or the mother's male partner, the mother's social and emotional adjustment, her childrearing practices and the community and familial supports she had received since her baby's birth.

The third interview with the mother, when her child was about 3 years old, contained questions comparable to those asked at Time 1 and Time 2. The schedule also included questions about training techniques used with the child and the degree of strictness or permissiveness. To gauge the child's current adjustment, 129 true-false state-

18

ments from the Louisville Behavior Check List (2) were incorporated. Questions dealing with role strain and role identification (3) were also included.

In the interviews at Time 2 and Time 3, the mother was given two forms to check. One, the Rosenberg Self-Esteem Scale, (4) consists of 10 statements on which the mothers were asked to check on a four-point scale the degree to which they agreed or disagreed with each statement. The second form, the Thomas-Zander Ego Strength Scale, (5) consisted of 27 statements that could be checked as true or false.

In all three interviews, six questions that correlate highly with the psychiatric evaluation of lower income families were also used (6). These questions had been used in an earlier followup study of unmarried mothers who had kept their children (7). The object was to determine not only the effects of psychiatric impairment on both the mother's and child's outcome measures, but whether psychiatric impairment was subject to change during the early childrearing years, and how the psychiatric impairment of these young mothers compared with that of mothers with older children.

Inperson interviews were the sole source of data obtained at Time 1. These interviews were conducted by interviewers employed by the project. At Time 2, a brief mail questionnaire incorporating some of the questions from the interview schedules was sent to mothers who were not geographically accessible. At Time 3, the mobility of these women meant that there might be considerable sample loss if interviewing was limited to mothers who remained in the Milwaukee area. Therefore, it was decided to include women who were not geographically accessible to the Milwaukee interviewing staff. Fortunately, the Child Welfare League has conducted research studies in other areas and it was possible to use former interviewers in these locales. Also, interviewers with experience in social work, known personally to staff members of the study, were used. Where no known local interviewer was available, a telephone interview was conducted.

19

COORDINATION AND INTERVIEWING

Since the field operations were in an area far from the research office, it was essential that a person in that area be responsible for coordination. An M.S.W. with extensive experience and wide acquaintance with both social work and hospital personnel in the area was hired. During the period in which mothers were being recruited through the hospitals and State Department, she maintained contact with the recruitment sources, collected the hospital consent forms, and reviewed these forms as well as the State Department forms, to eliminate women who, because of age or race, did not meet the study criteria.

Through the assistance of the Milwaukee County Department of Public Welfare and other local social agencies, five young women from the Milwaukee area were employed to conduct all of the interviews at Time 1. Two of these women held master's degrees in social work, and all had social work experience. Soon after the completion of the Time 1 interview, one interviewer moved; she was replaced by two others, both with experience in social work agencies. Generally, it was possible for the same interviewer to see the mother on at least two occasions, and more often, all three occasions. The maintenance of rapport between the interviewer and respondent through this 3-year period helped assure continued cooperation of many study subjects.

Prior to each interview, the study director met with the interviewers. The schedules were reviewed and role playing was used to familiarize the interviewers with the schedules. These training sessions gave the interviewers an understanding of the purpose of open-ended questions, and suggested other queries that might obtain pertinent responses. The feedback from these sessions also was helpful to the project director. Ambiguous questions were spotted and revised prior to the interviews.

INTERVIEWS AND ATTRITION BETWEEN TIME 1 AND TIME 3

The study began with a total of 448 women who had agreed to participate and who were interviewed soon after their baby's birth. Almost three-fifths (58%) of the mothers were married. Between the first interview and the final interviewing period, about 3 years later, three mothers died and five terminated parental rights to their children. This left a potential study population of 440--259 married and 181 unmarried women.

The stamina and personal investment of the interviewers is attested to by the high success rate in reaching these mothers at the two followup interviews. Although many of the women moved frequently, both within and outside the Milwaukee area, at Time 2 the interviewers conducted inperson interviews with 402 (91%) of the 440 mothers. An additional 20 women--5% of the total--were located in areas too distant from the interviewing site, and these women completed and returned the mail questionnaire. Thus, at Time 2, complete or partial data on 250 (97%) of the 259 married women and 172 (95%) of the 181 unmarried women were obtained.

At Time 3, about 3 years after the initial interview, 411 (93%) of the 440 mothers were located. Included were 245 (95%) of the 259 married women and 166 (92%) of the 181 unmarried women. Also known were the whereabouts of two other children born to unmarried women. With rare exceptions, an inperson interview was conducted with the mother. In a few instances (16) the mother had moved to an area in which there was no available interviewer, and a telephone interview was conducted. There was one instance in which the child, for whom the mother still maintained legal responsiblity, was being cared for by the maternal grandmother, and information about the child's adjustment, therefore, was obtained from the grandmother.

21

REPRESENTATIVENESS OF THE STUDY POPULATION

A. Cases Lost Because of Mother's Death or Relinquishment of Parental Rights

Eight cases were lost to the study because the mother died or surrendered her child for adoption. Two of the three mothers who died had been married at the time of their baby's birth. All three women were 20 years of age or older. Their deaths occurred between 6 months and 2 years after the baby's birth.

The five mothers who originally said they were keeping their children but later decided against it were, with one exception, under 17 years old at the time they gave birth. The youngest was 15½ and the oldest was 22. All made the decision to surrender before the child was 1 year old, and usually the surrender occurred within the first 6 months.

Unlike the majority of unwed mothers who continued to keep their children, these five mothers had discussed the possibility of adoption during their pregnancies, and usually this discussion was initiated by the young mother's parents. Only one mother had considered abortion, but had ruled against it. Parental pressure to surrender the child was evident in three of the five cases.

Two of the five mothers took their child with them at hospital discharge. These two teen-agers each went to live with the baby's paternal grandparents, since their own parents would not let them bring the baby into their home. In both instances the baby's father was living elsewhere. Inability to manage financially resulted in the return of one mother to her parents' home and the baby's placement in temporary foster care. The mother visited for a while, but before the child's first birthday she permanently terminated custody.

The second mother had known the father of her baby for several years and they planned to marry as soon as she became 16. Four months after the baby's birth their relationship ended. She continued living with his parents, who remained supportive of her plans to rear her child without the help of a husband. However, 2 months later she terminated custody: "I am just too young--I didn't realize what I was getting into."

The babies of the three other mothers went immediately to foster homes upon discharge from the hospital. One mother, who saw her baby only once while in the hospital, terminated custody after 3 months. The other two had their babies returned to them after about a month. One of these was the only mother who received any parental support. However, both mothers opted for adoption before the child was 6 months old. As the 22-year-old mother put it, "I just couldn't hack it."

B. Cases Lost Through Refusals or Inability to Locate

Data on those women who subsequently refused to cooperate in the study and those who could not be located are minimal. No data are available on those women who were never approached while in hospital or those who refused to sign a consent form. There is, therefore, no way of assessing the representativeness of the women who were interviewed, relative to all white primiparas under 25 years of age who delivered in Milwaukee hospitals during the recruitment period. Information about the socioeconomic status of patients generally served by the cooperating hospitals gives reason to believe that the married women in the study were perhaps of a slightly lower socioeconomic background than may have been true for all white primiparas under 25 years of age delivering in the hospitals in the area at that time.

A further question of representativeness relates to those 29 women who could not be located at Time 3. Since the study's married and unmarried populations differed on several variables, separate analyses were undertaken of the 14 married and the 15 unmarried women who were interviewed at Time 1 but not at Time 3, and comparisons with the other interviewed mothers in their respective groups were made.

Cross-tabulations were obtained on more than 75 variables on which the mothers located at Time 3 could have differed from those who were not located. These included social and economic characteristics of the mothers and their extended and nuclear families, their relationships within the home and community, and their supports, as well as a variety of attitudinal factors that they reported at the Time 1 interview. Among the married women a significant difference at the .01 level was found on one variable--about twice the proportion of married women who were not located at Time 3 were under 21 years of age at the time of their baby's birth. Two other items approached significance. A larger proportion of the married women not located had known their husband a shorter time (under 4 years) than had the married women who were interviewed. In addition, the incomes of the unlocated women were lower, with all but one reporting a monthly income under $700.

No significant differences were found among the unmarried women. However, as with the married women, a far larger proportion of the unmarried mothers who were not located at Time 3 had had a briefer acquaintanceship (under 2 years) with the baby's father than was true of those unmarried women who were located and interviewed. In addition, although the children of all of the Time 3 unmarried nonrespondents were living with them at Time 1, at Time 2 it was possible to ascertain that two of the children were in foster care.

It appears then that, with few exceptions, the 29 mothers who were excluded from the analyses of outcome were similar to the studied population. The women in the married population are older than would have been the case had all the married mothers at Time 3 been located. The married and unmarried women had somewhat longer acquaintanceship with the father of their child, and the married women were somewhat better off financially at Time 1 than would have been the case among married women had all mothers been located. Since the study controlled for both age and income in the analyses of outcome, any findings related to these variables may be generalizable to mothers seen at Time 1 as well as to the population at large.

24

CODING OPERATIONS AND STATISTICAL ANALYSIS OF DATA

Manuals were developed for coding of the data. To ensure reliability, all interviews were double-coded. In the relatively rare instances in which there was disagreement between coders with regard to the appropriate code, decisions were made in conference with the project director.

After entering the data on an SPSS system file, correlational analysis was used to combine related variables. So that no one item would receive disproportionate weight, Z scores were used in the development of each of the indices.

Each outcome variable was then cross-tabulated with each of the independent and intervening variables. Selected maternal characteristics* suggested by the study design as well as those variables on which differences were statistically significant at or beyond the .05 level, were included in the regression analysis in order to assess the relative influence of the independent and intervening variables on outcome for mother and child.

Since a hierarchical order for the independent variables was not assumed, a step-wise inclusion was utilized, in which the computer program ordered those variables that accounted for the greatest degree of variance on each test score.

---

* These included the mother's age at the time of her baby's birth, her marital and socioeconomic status at the onset of childrearing and at Times 2 and 3. The high correlation of age with education led to the exclusion of the latter variable from the regression analyses. Since cross-tabulation of the mothers' parents' socioeconomic status showed this variable to have little or no association with the outcome variables, it was also excluded. A similar decision was made in the case of the mother's early childhood experiences on the basis that cross-tabulation of this index with the outcome variables yielded no usefulness for analytic purposes.

25

REFERENCES

1. Kahn, Alfred, J. "The Design of Research," in Polansky, editor, Social Work Research. Chicago: University of Chicago Press, 1960, 52-54.

2. Miller, Lovick C. Louisville Behavior Check List Manual. Louisville: Department of Psychiatry, School of Medicine, University of Louisville.

3. Nye, Ivan F., and Gegas, Victor. Family Analysis: The Washington Family Role Inventory. College of Agriculture Research Center, Washington State University, Technical Bulletin 82, January 1976.

4. Robinson, John P., and Shaver, Philip R. Measures of Social Psychological Attitudes, Ann Arbor, Michigan: Survey Research Center, Institute for Social Research, 1973.

5. Ibid.

6. Langner, Thomas S., et al. "Psychiatric Impairment in Welfare and Non-Welfare Children," Welfare in Review. 7, 2 (March-April 1969), 10-21.

7. Sauber, Mignon, and Corrigan, Eileen M. The Six-Year Experience of Unwed Mothers as Parents. New York: Community Council of Greater New York, 1970.

CHAPTER 3
SOCIAL CHARACTERISTICS OF THE MOTHERS

Data obtained at Time 1 on the initial study population are presented in this and the following chapter. As stated earlier, the Time 1 interview with the 448 mothers occurred soon after the baby's birth. In this chapter the mothers' age, living arrangements, income, educational and occupational background, and health are described. Data concerning the families of the mothers as well as information about the fathers of the babies also are presented. A summary of the data obtained at Time 1 can be found in Chapter 4.

Since a major concern is the potential for differing outcome between married and unmarried mothers, in Chapters 3 through 7 any differences by marital status that are significant at the .01 level or beyond are reported. Characterized as "unmarried" are 187 women who had never been married at the time of the baby's birth, even though four were married by the time of the first interview and others married subsequently. Also, designated as "married" are the 261 women who were identified as married when they were screened into the study, although eight of these women were either separated or divorced at the time their baby was born.

AGE AND LIVING ARRANGEMENTS

At the time of their baby's birth the age of the mothers ranged from 14 years (two mothers) to 25 (one mother),*

---

* It was not learned until after the Time 1 interview was conducted that this woman was past the study's age limit. Since the difference was a matter of a few months, it was decided to retain her in the study.

with a median of 20.4. Sixteen percent of the mothers were under 18 and 42% were between 18 and 20. The unmarried women were considerably younger; a third were under 18, in contrast to 5% of the married women. The median age of the married women was 21.7; the median age for the unmarried women was 18.9 (Table 3-1).

Only two of the married women had been married previously. About a third of the married mothers had conceived this first-born child prior to marriage and over a fourth were at least 3 months pregnant at the time they married. The age of the mothers at the time of the current marriage ranged from 15 years (two mothers) to 24 (one mother). Two-thirds were under 21 when they married their current spouses. The median age at the time of the current marriage was 19.9 years* (Table 3-2).

Seventy-one percent of the married women, as compared with 10% of the unmarried women, were living with the baby's father at the time they became pregnant. About a fourth of the married and almost two-thirds of the unmarried women lived with their parents. The rest--5% of the married women and 27% of the unmarried--lived either alone, with friends, relatives, in college dorms or the like.

During the pregnancy, living arrangements changed considerably. Almost all the married women (93%) began living with the baby's father; the rest either lived with their parents or lived alone. Three-fifths of the unmarried women stayed in their parents' home during their pregnancy. Less than a tenth (8%) lived with the baby's father. Most of the others either lived alone (12%) or moved in with friends (10%). A few entered a maternity or a foster home. One unmarried woman "lived on the street," as she put it.

The first interview usually occurred from 2 to 4 weeks after the baby's birth. At that point almost all of

---

* The fact that this study population was restricted to primiparous women under 25 accounts for the younger age at marriage of the women in this study. In the years 1970-1973 the median age for first marriage for all women ranged from 20.8 to 21.0. Statistical Abstract of the U.S. 1974. Table No. 93, p. 66.

Table 3-1

Mother's Age at Baby's Birth

Percentage Distribution

Age	Married (N=261)	Unmarried (N=187)	Total (N=448)
Under 18	5	33	16
18	11	17	13
19	10	17	13
20	16	15	16
21	10	8	9
22	15	4	10
23 and above	33	6	23
Total	100	100	100
Median	21.7	18.9	20.4

$x^2 = 109.42$, 6 d.f., p less than .001

Table 3-2

Age at Time of Current Marriage

Percentage Distribution (Married Women Only)

Age	(N=261)
Under 18	10
18	19
19	20
20	17
21	19
22 and above	15
Total	100
Median	19.9

the married mothers (97%) were living with a male partner (in all but one instance, the husband). Eighty-seven percent lived in the typical nuclear two-parent family unit of husband, wife and child. Those who lived with relatives or friends usually regarded this as temporary until they could find more adequate living quarters.

On the other hand, over two-fifths (44%) of the unmarried women lived with one or both of their parents. More than a fifth (23%) had no adults living with them. A tenth of the mothers lived with a male partner who, with one exception, was the baby's father. A few mothers (2%) had married and were living with their husbands. The others usually lived with other relatives or, in a few instances, friends. Unlike the married women, these mothers usually regarded their living arrangements with relatives or friends as permanent. For the unmarried women the median number of persons living in the home was 5.82; for the married, it was 3.45.

HOUSING

A majority of the mothers (81%) considered the physical and structural aspects of their living accommodations to be adequate. Despite the generally greater number of persons in the unmarried women's homes, the differences in the assessment of married and unmarried mothers were minimal. It may well be that overcrowding, the problem most frequently mentioned by those who deemed their living accommodations inadequate, was outweighed by the assistance the mothers could anticipate in caring for infants.

Children of the married women were far more likely to have a bedroom of their own--about two-thirds (64%) versus a fifth (18%) of the children of the unmarried mothers. In those instances in which children shared the bedroom with somebody else, it was generally with the child's mother or both parents. In the case of four unmarried mothers, a lack of space and furniture necessitated their babies' sharing the bed with them.

INCOME

A majority of the women reported no such worry, but about one of every six mothers (16%) said they had been worried about their financial plight at the time of their hospital discharge. A tenth (9%) of the married women, as compared with a fourth of the unmarried women, reported this to be the case.

However, the initial handicap for parent and child among the unmarried mothers is evident. Almost half of the unmarried women about whom such information was obtained were expected to support themselves and, in most cases, their children on monthly incomes of less than $200. Only about a tenth (11%) of them had monthly incomes of $400 or more, in contrast to nine-tenths of the married women. The median monthly income for the married women was $675.49, as against $216.10 for the unmarried women (Table 3-3).

Table 3-3

Monthly Income at Time 1

Percentage Distribution

Income	Married (N=246)	Unmarried (N=172)	Total* (N=418)
Under $200	2	49	21
$200-399	8	40	21
$400-599	28	4	18
$600-799	29	6	20
$800- and above	33	1	20
Total	100	100	100
Median Monthly Income	$675.49	$216.10	$538.64

x^2 = 264.66, 4 d.f., p less than .001

*No information on 15 married and 15 unmarried women

Despite the less than adequate income of at least half of the unmarried women, their optimistic outlook is shown in their responses to a question whether they thought that, in the view of the expense, this was a good or bad time for them to have had a baby. Only a third (34%) of the unmarried women saw the time as bad. The responses of the married women seemed more reflective of their higher incomes, since only 12% had questions about the timing.

SOCIAL CHARACTERISTICS OF THE MOTHERS' FAMILIES

Over four-fifths of the parents of these women were born in Wisconsin or a contiguous state. A few parents (4%) were born outside the United States. Since nine-tenths of the women in the study were also born and reared in Wisconsin or its environs, it appears that they came from families of relatively low geographic mobility.

About two-thirds of the women's parents on whom such information was available had completed high school or a more advanced level of education. The parents of the unmarried mothers were somewhat less well educated than those of the married mothers, and the difference in educational attainment between the fathers of the married and unmarried women is significant (Table 3-4).

Table 3-4

Educational and Occupational Background
of Mothers' Fathers

Education	Married (N=261)	Unmarried (N=187)	Total (N=448)
8th grade or less	16%	18%	17%
9th-11th grade	14	27	19
High school graduate	41	38	40
Some college or technical training	16	10	13
College graduate	13	7	11
Total	100	100	100
No information	8	18	12

$x^2 = 14.83$, 4 d.f., p less than .01

Occupation

Unskilled laborer	5%	5%	5%
Farmer	2	1	1
Service	6	5	6
Semiskilled	22	25	23
Skilled	23	33	27
Clerical and sales	13	10	12
Managers, officials, proprietors	19	14	17
Professional, technical	10	7	9
Total	100	100	100
No information	5	10	7

$$x^2 = 6.97, \ 6 \ d.f., \ N.S.$$

Almost two-fifths of their mothers had never held outside employment. The most usual employment of the fathers was in semiskilled or skilled jobs. Despite differences in educational attainment by the fathers, differences in parental occupation between the married and unmarried were minimal.

At the time the women were first interviewed nearly all of their mothers (96%) and most of their fathers (85%) were alive. Although there had been more parental loss through death among the unmarried mothers, the differences were not significant. The mothers of a few of the women had never married. Others were separated, divorced or remarried. In the case of about three-fourths (73%) of the women, however, there had been no marital disruption in the parental home. More of the married women came from homes in which the parental marriage had remained intact than was true for the unmarried group --78% versus 65% (Table 3-5).

About three-fifths of the mothers described the relationship between their parents as good. A fourth described it as average and the rest as poor. The married mothers were much more likely to assess the parental relationship positively--70% describing it as good, versus 45% of the unmarried mothers.

Table 3-5
Selected Descriptive Characteristics
of Mother's Childhood

Parent's Marital Status	Married (N=261)	Unmarried (N=187)	Total (N=448)
Married, living together	78%	65%	73%
Separated, divorced, one or both deceased	21	33	25
Never married	1	2	2
Total	100	100	100

x^2 = 9.84, 1 d.f., p less than .01

Parental Relationship			
Good	70	45	59
Average	20	31	25
Poor	10	24	16
Total	100	100	100
No information, no couple	3	5	4

x^2 = 29.60, 2 d.f., p less than .001

Number of Siblings			
None	6	3	4
One	13	8	11
Two	23	15	20
Three	19	23	21
Four	14	18	16
Five or more	25	33	28
Total	100	100	100
No information	–	1	–
Median	3.45	4.85	3.62

x^2 = 10.86, 1 d.f., p less than .001

Changes in Parental Authority Figures			
None	82	68	76
One	12	19	14
Two or more	6	13	10
Total	100	100	100

x^2 = 11.36, 2 d.f., p less than .01

Relationship With Father

Close	76%	56%	67%
So-so	15	19	17
Distant	9	25	16
Total	100	100	100
No information, no father or father substitute	4	3	3

x^2 = 22.54, 2 d.f., p less than .001

Relationship With Mother

Close	83	69	77
So-so	10	20	14
Distant	7	11	9
Total	100	100	100
No mother or mother substitute	-	1	-

x^2 = 14.25, 2 d.f., p less than .001

Most (95%) of the mothers had one or more siblings. The married mothers tended to have fewer siblings, with 42% of them coming from homes in which there were three or fewer children, as compared with only 26% of the unmarried women. With few exceptions, if siblings existed, mothers reported a close relationship with one or more of them.

A majority of the mothers had the same parental authority figures throughout their childhood, but about a fourth of the women had undergone changes in parental authority figures. Most frequently the change involved the absence of one parent because of divorce or separation. Changes sometimes occurred because of a parent's death. In a few instances the parents delegated childrearing to other family members. Whereas less than a fifth (18%) of the married mothers had one or more changes in parental authority figures, this was true for a third (32%) of the unmarried mothers.

In the majority of cases the relationship between the mother and her parents was positive. Two-thirds of the women described their relationship with their father as close--76% of the married, but only 56% of the unmarried. An even larger proportion (77%) described a close relationship with their mother--83% of the married, versus 69% of the unmarried women.

EDUCATIONAL AND OCCUPATIONAL BACKGROUND

About two-thirds of the women had not been attending school within the year prior to their baby's birth--77% of the married and 47% of the unmarried women. Some had graduated; others were dropouts. The proportion of women who had quit school prior to high school graduation was considerably higher among the unmarried--over a third (35%)--as compared with a seventh (14%) of the married women.

Of the 158 women who were in school that year, two-fifths reported that they eventually left because of their pregnancy. Fifteen mothers, including one who was married, continued on in regular school during their pregnancy. Twenty-three mothers, two of whom were married, were tutored or else attended special classes for pregnant women. Most of the women--both married and unmarried--who left school because of pregnancy said they planned to return soon to complete their education.

By the time of the first interview, nearly three-fourths of the mothers had completed high school, and almost a third had obtained further education following high school. Since the unmarried women tended to be younger, it is not surprising that they also had less education on the whole than the married women. Almost half (45%) had not completed high school, in contrast to about a sixth (16%) of the married women (Table 3-6).

Most of the women--96% of the married and 80% of the unmarried--had worked at some point prior to the birth of their babies. Occupations varied from service work (22%) to professional and technical work (6%), but the majority held clerical or sales jobs. In most instances the women had worked no longer than 2 years. Over a third had worked a year or less.

Table 3-6

Amount of Schooling at Time 1

Educational Level	Married (N=261)	Unmarried* (N=286)	Total (N=447)
9th grade or less	2%	12%	6%
10th-11th grade	14	33	22
High school graduate	40	43	42
Some college or technical training	36	11	25
College graduate	8	1	5
Total	100	100	100

$$x^2 = 45.28, \text{ 2 d.f., p less than .001}$$

*No information on one unmarried woman

Three-fourths of the women held jobs during part or all of their pregnancy--80% of the married and 70% of the unmarried mothers. Although a fourth of the women quit employment during the first 3 months, almost half (46%) continued working into the third trimester. A few mothers stopped working only during their actual confinement and for perhaps a few days before and after (Table 3-7).

Table 3-7

Trimester in Which Working Mothers Terminated Employment

Trimester	Married (N=261)	Unmarried (N=187)	Total (N=448)
First	20%	33%	25%
Second	26	33	29
Third, Never	54	34	46
Total	100	100	100
Not employed	20	30	24

$$x^2 = 13.74, \text{ 2 d.f., p less than .01}$$

The married women stayed at their jobs longer than did the unmarried women. In the past, societal attitudes toward the unmarried pregnant woman frequently pressured her into leaving her job prematurely. If the reasons the mothers gave for leaving their job are accepted at face value, such pressure no longer appears to exist. Only one woman (unmarried) reported that she left because she was "embarrassed," and equal proportions of married and unmarried were required to leave by their employer. On the other hand, a third of the unmarried women, as compared with only a fifth of the married women, said they stopped working because they did not feel well, the work was too strenuous, or their doctor had recommended quitting--reasons that may have camouflaged embarrassment over being pregnant and unmarried.

At the time of the first interview almost half (46%) of the women had returned to work or expected to be working within the year. Early employment was much more likely for the unmarried than the married--56% versus 38%. Of those women not expecting to work within the year, most did not intend to seek outside employment in the foreseeable future, although a few (6%) said that they might do so at some point, such as when their child reached school age.

For those who were employed or expected to be employed soon, arrangements for child care were usually with the maternal grandmother, although this was true much more frequently in the case of the unmarried women. The next most usual resource was the baby's father, true for a sizable proportion of the married women, but for only a few of the unmarried. Other relatives were mentioned next as a frequent or expected source of baby care help, the proportions being about the same for both married and unmarried. Only a few women mentioned paid babysitters or friends and neighbors as providing substitute care while they worked. On the other hand, there was a sizable number of mothers, with similar proportions of married and unmarried women, who intended to seek outside employment but had not yet found someone to care for their infant.

38

Three-fourths of the women said they had had no physical problems, or else only minor problems common to most pregnant women (e.g., heartburn, constipation, etc.) during their pregnancy. Indeed, few women reported any special restrictions having been prescribed during this period. About a fifth (19%) were advised to follow special diets and a small number were told to exercise or, conversely, to cut down on their activities. In those instances where special instructions were given, most mothers reported having followed them.

On the other hand, when presented with a list of possible symptoms that the expectant mother might have in the beginning, middle, end, or throughout her pregnancy, a sizable proportion of women reported having had such symptoms. Seventy-three percent reported having felt fatigue at one point or throughout their pregnancy. Married women reported this symptom more frequently. Nausea was experienced by two-thirds of the women and by equal proportions of both groups. Irritability and depression were experienced by over half the women, with proportionately more of the unwed women enduring these symptoms throughout pregnancy. Food fads, backaches or leg cramps and headaches were problems that over a fourth to less than half of all the mothers experienced and, with the exception of food fads, these symptoms rarely occurred throughout the pregnancy. Thus, only on three symptoms were differences found between married and unmarried women. More married women reported fatigue; more unmarried reported being irritable and depressed throughout their pregnancy (Table 3-8).

About a fourth of the women described other discomforts during their pregnancy. Generally these were minor gastro-intestinal disorders or discomfort because of the size or position of the baby.

Postpartum crying was experienced by about half (53%) of the women. Usually this was after the mother's discharge from the hospital. (At the Time 1 interview a tenth of the women who had had this symptom were still experiencing it.)

39

Table 3-8

Symptoms During Pregnancy

Percentage Reporting*

	At One Point		
Symptoms	Married	Unmarried	Total
Nausea	56	56	56
Headaches	19	19	19
Fatigue	56	38	48
Irritability	36	32	34
Depression	38	26	33
Food Fads	20	19	19
Backaches, leg cramps	26	31	28

	Throughout				
Symptoms	Married	Unmarried	Total	x^2**	P
Nausea	9	9	9	0.00	N.S.
Headaches	10	9	9	0.01	N.S.
Fatigue	22	28	20	14.13	.001
Irritability	14	28	20	14.59	.001
Depression	10	32	19	36.35	.001
Food fads	24	31	27	3.41	N.S.
Backaches, leg cramps	9	11	10	1.93	N.S.

*n = 261 married and 187 unmarried women
**d.f. = 2 "never," "at one point," "throughout"

In general, these mothers appeared to be relatively healthy. At the first interview, the majority (88%) reported their physical health as either excellent or good. If health problems were mentioned, they were usually identified as anemia, headaches, backaches or general fatigue. Most of the women (87%) either already had or planned to have a medical checkup.

To evaluate their emotional health, the mothers were asked six questions concerning possible symptoms and

40

complaints (1). On all but two of the items, four-fifths or more of the mothers reported no problems or complaints. On the other hand, almost half of the women complained of an inability "to get going" (lassitude) and almost a fourth of the total group complained of feeling isolated. In the case of isolation, the differences between married and unmarried are significant, the unmarried mothers reporting this feeling far more often than the married mothers.

The responses of the study mothers were compared with Langner's study on mothers on welfare (2) and with the Sauber-Corrigan study of mothers unmarried at the time of their baby's birth (3). With the exception of a feeling of lassitude, for the total group in the current study and among the married women in particular, there were fewer symptoms of psychiatric impairment. On the other hand, the unmarried women in the current study differed from the other mothers in only three of the six measures. They had fewer symptoms of depression and weakness than did the women in the two other studies; they also indicated less restlessness than did the women in the earlier unmarried mothers' study. The proportions of unwed mothers reporting feelings of isolation, lassitude, and nervousness were similar to the proportions who had reported these symptoms in the two earlier studies (Table 3-9).

THE FATHERS OF THE BABIES

At the time of the baby's birth, the fathers' ages ranged from 17 to 56. About a third were under 21, over half were between 21 and 27, and the rest were 27 or older. The median age was 22.8. As expected, fathers of the unmarried mothers' children were younger. Half of these men were under 21, while this was true for only a fifth of the fathers of children whose mothers were married (Table 3-10).

Education ranged from less than high school to college graduation, with more than three-fourths of the men having a high school diploma. Since they were older, educational attainment of men in the married group was higher. At the mothers' first interview, about a fifth of the

Table 3-9

Psychiatric Impairment

Percentage Reporting Symptoms

	Current Study Married (N=261)	Current Study Unmarried (N=187)	Current Study Total (N=448)	Sauber-Corrigan Unmarried Mothers (N=205)	Langner, et al. (Low Income Mothers) (N=126)
Symptoms					
Restlessness	20^{ab}	20^{a}	20^{ab}	37	33
Isolation*	18^{ab}	29_{ab}	23^{ab}	33	35
Weakness	11^{ab}	12^{ab}	11^{ab}	23	29
Lassitude	42_{ab}	50	45_{ab}	42	43
Nervousness	12^{ab}	17_{ab}	14^{ab}	26	20
Depression	3^{ab}	6^{ab}	4^{ab}	21	16

a   Difference between current study mothers and Sauber-Corrigan mothers significant at or beyond .01

ab Difference between current study mothers and mothers in two other studies significant at or beyond .01

*   Differences between married and unmarried mothers in current study: x^2 = 11.14, 1 d.f., p less than .001

Table 3-10

Age of Baby's Father

Age	Married (N=261)	Unmarried (N=182)	Total (N=443)
Under 18	--%	12%	5%
18-20	20	39	27
21-23	32	21	28
24-26	31	16	25
27-29	12	4	9
30 and above	5	8	6
Total	100	100	100
Median	23.7	20.9	22.8

x^2 = 66.85, 5 d.f., p less than .001

*no information on age of baby's father in the case of five unmarried women.

children's fathers were still attending school, with a similar proportion in both groups. The school dropout rate--that is, the proportion of fathers who had not completed high school and who were no longer attending school--was considerably higher among the unmarried--35% versus 16% in the married group.

Most of the men were employed, and usually (for two-fifths of the total group) in a semiskilled job. Since the fathers of the children whose mothers were married tended to be older and better educated, it was not surprising that a much higher proportion of these men, as compared with the fathers in the unmarried group, held professional or technical jobs--23% versus 8%.

The majority (93%) of the men were white. This was true for 98% of the fathers of children whose mothers were married, but for only 86% of those in the unmarried group. Usually the nonwhite father was black or, less frequently, American Indian.

In most instances--in all but 4% of the cases--this was the first marriage for the fathers of children whose mothers were married at the time of their baby's birth. Among the unmarried, three-fourths of the babies' fathers were reported to be single and 16% were separated or divorced. The others, with the exception of five cases in which the unmarried mother did not know the father's marital status, were married to someone other than the mother of the child in this study.

During the first interview, mothers were asked how long they had been acquainted with the baby's father. Seven percent had known the baby's father about 3 months or less prior to conception. This was true for 2% of the married and 14% of the unmarried women. About half (49%) of the mothers and fathers had had no more than a 15-month acquaintance prior to the baby's conception--32% of the married and 73% of the unmarried parents. At the other extreme were those couples (28% of the total) who had been acquainted for more than 4 years--41% of the married, but only 10% of the unmarried.

All but seven of the married women were receiving financial support from the baby's father. The seven were either separated or divorced from their husbands who, with three exceptions, were reported to be the baby's father. Five of the seven fathers had separated from their wives during the pregnancy and had not been in touch with the mother since the baby's birth, even though they knew of the baby's existence and, in four instances, acknowledged paternity. Four of these wives either had taken legal action to obtain support or were planning to do so.

The fathers of two children born to unmarried mothers had died. Well over a third (37%) of the others were providing some financial support, even though it was usually sporadic. Of those few who were supporting regularly, the median weekly payment was $17.50. Legal action for support had either been completed or been initiated in 27% of the cases, and in another 12% legal action was being considered. The most frequent reason given for not taking legal action was that the father was providing at least some support voluntarily. Additional reasons, in descending order of frequency, were to avoid embarrassment, because the mother saw financial support as her sole responsibility, because she knew the baby's father couldn't afford payments, or because the mother did not want him to know of the baby's existence. Among this unmarried group, 9% of the men were unaware of the baby's birth. An additional 16% knew about the baby but did not acknowledge paternity.

When the mothers were asked to describe the father's attitude, in most instances (83%) the father was said to be very pleased or somewhat pleased about having the child. This response was given by almost all (96%) of the married women, but by only about two-thirds (64%) of the unmarried mothers.

The advent of a baby into a couple's life can have a beneficial, innocuous or sometimes detrimental effect on the parental relationship. Among the mothers in this study all three effects were reported, although negative consequences were more frequently the case among the unmarried. The baby's birth was reported to have brought couples closer in over two-fifths (44%) of the cases--55% of the married couples but only 29% of the unmarried. For over a

44

third (35%) there was said to be no change and in the rest the couples were said to be less close or to have terminated their relationship--7% of the married couples and 42% of the unmarried.

COMMITMENT TO MARRIAGE--THE UNWED MOTHER

What plans did the unwed mother have with regard to marrying the father of their baby? In general, how committed were they to legitimating their baby's birth through marriage? Three-fifths (61%) of the unmarried women, including six of the 18 women who were living with the fathers of their babies, said they had no plans to marry the baby's father and a tenth said they were still unsure. Among those with definite plans to marry, all but one planned to marry the putative father, and the intention of more than half was to marry within the year.

Whether or not they had intentions of marrying, more than three-fifths (62%) of the unmarried women indicated some commitment to marriage, even if only for the sake of the baby; on the other hand, 19% said that being married or unmarried was immaterial and 9% indicated that it was better to remain single. The women who expressed neutrality or opposition to marriage viewed the legal status for mother and child as unimportant, did not believe pregnancy a sufficient reason for marriage and spoke of the instability of today's marriages.

NOTES AND REFERENCES

1. Langner, Thomas S., et al. "Psychiatric Impairment in Welfare and Non-Welfare Children," Welfare in Review, 7, 2 (March-April 1969), pp. 10-21.

2. Ibid.

3. At the time the study was conducted the children were 6 years old. About half the mothers had subsequently married and 28% were living with their husbands at the time of the interview. Sauber,

Mignon, and Corrigan, Eileen M., The Six-Year Experience of Unwed Mothers as Parents, Community Council of Greater New York, 1970.

CHAPTER 4
PRENATAL EXPERIENCES, SUPPORTS, THE CHILDREN
AND THEIR CARE

This chapter describes additional data obtained from the mothers at the interview shortly after the baby's birth. Information concerning the mothers' prenatal experiences and care and data on the children and their care are reported. Also included are the mothers' actual and potential supports in fulfilling their child care role, the mothers' use of community services and the interviewers' observations of the mothers and their care of their children.

PRENATAL EXPERIENCES

Generally this was the mother's first pregnancy. A few (7%) had been pregnant previously, usually within 2 years of the current pregnancy. In all but four instances the pregnancies terminated in miscarriages. Two mothers obtained abortions; the other two pregnancies ended in still-births.

Over two-thirds (69%) of the mothers had had no sex information courses in school. Among those who did about two-thirds reported the courses as instructive. All but 7% of the women--96% of the married and 88% of· the unmarried mothers--knew about contraceptives prior to their pregnancy. This knowledge usually had been obtained through friends or reading matter (44%) or else through their physician or family planning clinic (40%). Only 11%, with similar proportions of married and unmarried, had learned about contraceptive devices from their parents. The rest received their information from the baby's father.

Sixty-eight percent of the pregnancies were un-planned, with unplanned pregnancies more common among the unmarried than the married women. Two-fifths of the women with unplanned pregnancies said they had "taken measures" to avoid becoming pregnant. Over half of these mothers had thought themselves sufficiently protected by abstaining from intercourse during what they thought was their fertility period (1). Less than a third had used contraceptive devices and an even smaller proportion had used the pill. Four unmarried women thought they were safe by having sex infrequently and two said they had been raped.

A fourth of the women whose pregnancy was not planned, and who hadn't tried to avoid pregnancy, reported that they had had no objection to becoming pregnant. This was the response of two-fifths of the married women and about a tenth (12%) of the unmarried. Seventeen percent of the mothers, a higher proportion of unmarried than married, said they had either no access to or else no information about contraceptives. Another 14% had apparently had the attitude of "It can't happen to me"--that is, they thought themselves too young to become pregnant, or "I didn't become pregnant before so I won't become pregnant now." Other reasons given for not trying to avoid pregnancy were dislike of contraceptives (11%), a lack of forethought about the consequences of intercourse expressed in such statements as "I just never thought of that possibility" (10%), and intercourse on impulse (9%). In addition, there were some women who believed it wrong to use contraceptives and there were a few who had not protected themselves because their partner objected.

Among those who reported that their pregnancy was planned, over two-fifths (44%) of the married women said they felt it was "time to have a family." An additional fifth reasoned that they were now "financially able" to have a child. A few married mothers said their intention in becoming pregnant was to improve their marital relationship (three mothers) or to force a marriage with their boyfriend (three).

The unmarried woman who said her pregnancy was planned most always said that she wanted a baby fathered by the particular man, or else hoped that a pregnancy would result in marriage to the baby's father.

48

Awareness of pregnancy ranged from "immediately" to just prior to the baby's birth (one mother). Almost half (46%) of the women said they knew they were pregnant within the first month. By the end of the second month, 84% of the mothers were aware of their condition--89% of the married women but only 77% of the unmarried.

For most of the women the first person in whom they confided about the pregnancy was the baby's father. This was true for 84% of the married but for only 48% of the unmarried women. Over a fourth of the unmarried women (28%) but only 6% of the married first confided in a friend. The first confidant for relatively few was a parent (7%) or other relative (7%), with the unmarried mothers turning to these sources more frequently than the married mothers.

Three-fourths of the women--87% of the married but only 57% of the unmarried--sought prenatal care in the first trimester. By the end of the second trimester all but one married and 13 unmarried women were receiving prenatal care (Table 4-1). One 21-year-old unmarried woman, a high school graduate, who suspected that she was pregnant but was unable to confide in anyone, did not receive medical supervision until her hospital admission for delivery. The majority of the women--79% of the married but only 64% of the unmarried--received prenatal medical supervision from a private physician.

Table 4-1
Trimester in Which Prenatal Care Began

Trimester	Married (N=261)	Unmarried (N=187)	Total (N=448)
First	87%	57%	74%
Second	13	36	23
Third, Never	-	7	3
Total	100	100	100

$$x^2 = 54.24, \text{ 2 d.f., p less than } .001$$

The mothers were given a list of initial reactions they might have on first learning they were pregnant and were asked whether any applied to them. Almost two-thirds (64%) of the mothers--77% of the married but only 47% of the unmarried women--said their reaction was one of happiness. About a third said they had been worried, and a similar proportion said they had been scared. Reactions of confusion or of being generally upset were reported less frequently, each by about a fifth of the women. A tenth of the mothers said they had been depressed. In each instance unmarried mothers reported more negative reactions than did married mothers (Table 4-2).

Table 4-2
Mother's Reaction Upon Learning About Pregnancy
Percentage Reporting

Reactions	Married (N=261)	Unmarried (N=187)	Total (N=448)	x^2	p
Happy	77	47	64	41.58	.001
Scared	22	41	30	17.56	.001
Depressed	5	20	11	21.05	.001
Worried	21	48	32	35.05	.001
Confused	14	31	21	17.49	.001
Upset	13	27	19	12.55	.001

Feelings about pregnancy and about motherhood can be qualitatively different, though both are biological events, and evidence suggests that women do not always connect pregnancy with having a baby (2). Therefore, later in the interview a second question was asked: After becoming pregnant, how did she feel about the prospect of having a baby? Two-fifths (41%) of the women said they were very pleased. This was the response of more than half (56%) of the married women but only a fifth (21%) of the unmarried. About a fourth (24%) said they were somewhat pleased. The others--a fifth of the married but half (52%) of the unmarried--expressed feelings of ambivalence or displeasure.

When the mothers' statements on reactions to being pregnant were compared with their statements regarding the prospect of having a baby, it was apparent that pregnancy and impending motherhood were indeed regarded differently by many of these women. About half (48%) of the married women but only a third (34%) of the unmarried who reported being unhappy about being pregnant expressed pleasure at the idea of having a baby. On the other hand, well over a third (36%) of the unmarried but only 13% of the married women who said they were ambivalent or displeased at the prospect of becoming a mother said that they were happy when they first learned they were pregnant. The responses of the married women were significantly more consistent--i.e., happy to be pregnant and pleased to become a mother; unhappy to be pregnant and ambivalent or displeased about becoming a mother. For 79% of the married women but only 65% of the unmarried their initial feelings about pregnancy and their feelings about having a child were in agreement (Table 4-3).

Table 4-3
Consistency of Responses to Feelings About Pregnancy and Motherhood
Percentage Distribution

Responses	Married (N=261)	Unmarried (N=186)*
Happy about pregnancy, pleased to become a mother	67	30
Unhappy about pregnancy, ambivalent or displeased to become a mother	12	35
Happy about pregnancy, ambivalent or displeased to become a mother	10	17
Unhappy about pregnancy, pleased to become a mother	11	18

Consistency (79% and 65%) versus inconsistency (21% and 35%)

x^2 = 9.94, 1 d.f., p less than .01

* Data not available for one unmarried woman

Even though over a third of these women had negative feelings upon learning of their pregnancy and were not particularly happy about the prospect of motherhood, only 14% said they had considered having an abortion--8% of the married and 22% of the unmarried women. However, about two-fifths (41%) of the unmarried women had thought about adoption. Well over half (56%) of those who had thought about it had talked with a social worker. Most of the others had discussed adoption only with their parents, although a few had talked about it with the baby's father, a friend, or a doctor or lawyer. At the Time 1 interview there were three unmarried women who still were undecided whether adoption might not be the best plan.

POTENTIAL AND ACTUAL EMOTIONAL SUPPORTS

About one of every 10 mothers--17% of the unmarried women but only 3% of the married mothers--said that at the time of their hospital discharge they had been worried about the reactions of their relatives and friends to their having had a baby. Nine of every 10 women, with similar proportions of married and unmarried, believed that their families had been supportive of them during their pregnancy. About eight of every 10 women felt that their friends had been helpful also. Over three-fourths of the mothers had found the baby's father supportive. Although emotional support from the baby's father was reported by almost all (96%) of the married women, only half (51%) of the unmarried women had found the baby's father helpful.

Very few of the mothers were members of clubs, associations or other organized or semiorganized groups. Less than a fifth participated in formal or semiformal group activities prior to the baby's birth and even fewer had plans for continuing with such activities afterward. Asked what they liked to do in their spare time, the women usually mentioned a combination of activities. Passive activities such as reading, watching television or the like, and creative activities such as knitting, drawing and painting, etc., were mentioned by about two-thirds of the

52

women. Less than half (46%) said that they preferred card playing, bowling and dancing--activities most likely to involve interaction with others.

On the other hand, most of the women reported having two or more close friends. Only a few (9%) reported having only one close friend; fewer (3%) said they had no friends. The unwed mother tended to report fewer friends, but the difference only approached statistical significance. In most instances the friend or friends lived nearby.

Almost half (47%) of the women reported that their neighbors were friendly, 28% described their relationship with neighbors as so-so, 20% reported their neighbors as being cool or distant and the rest were so new to their neighborhood that they were unable to offer an opinion. About two-fifths (38%) said that their neighbors visited them at least weekly and a slightly higher proportion said they also visited their neighbors in their homes.

THE CHILDREN

Almost three-fifths (57%) of the women said they had wanted to experience "natural childbirth," with a higher proportion of married women expressing this desire. However, only 44% of the women were able to deliver in this manner--49% of the married and 37% of the unmarried mothers. In most instances the mother's preference could not be accommodated because of medical complications or prematurity; sometimes, however, the physician did not agree to the mother's wish.

Four hundred and fifty-one babies, including three sets of male twins, were born to these mothers. Forty-five percent were female, a ratio somewhat lower than the national norm (3). Usually--in 85% of the deliveries--the birth was without complication. Five percent of the children were born prematurely. In 12% of the cases the delivery was by instrument or Caesarean section.

The majority of the babies (92%) returned home with their mothers at the time of the mother's discharge from the hospital. Twenty-one babies had to remain in the hospital because of low birth weight or other health problems; the babies of 10 unwed mothers went directly from the hospital to foster homes. By the time of the first interview all but eight children were with their mothers. The prematurely born infant of one married woman was still in the hospital. Six infants of unmarried mothers were in foster care; three of these children were surrendered for adoption shortly after placement. The eighth child, born to a 16-year-old unmarried woman, was living with a paternal aunt, since the maternal grandparents would not permit this child of mixed race in their home. The child's mother visited daily and participated in the infant's care.

In the period between discharge to mother and the Time 1 interview, 84% of the children remained in continuous care with their mothers. With the exception of nine instances in which the mother-child separation extended 2 weeks or longer, separations of mother and child were for no more than a week's duration. Usually the separation was just for a night or, at the most, a couple of days. The most frequent reasons given for a mother-child separation were to permit the mother freedom to relax or to take care of pressing needs. A few separations occurred because the mother was ill. During the mother's absence, most often the baby was cared for by the maternal grandmother, other relatives, or a close friend. In a few instances a mother employed someone to care for her baby during her absence.

Most of the children (91%) were reported to be in good health. In the case of those whose health was not good it was usually because of congenital defects. Other health complaints were that the baby was colicky, had asthma or other respiratory ailments, was underweight, had jaundice, or had sustained birth injuries.

At the time of the first interview, 89% of the babies had been seen for a posthospital medical checkup or else an appointment, usually with a pediatrician, had been arranged. Six percent of the married women were using a baby clinic for their infant's medical care, in contrast to 21% of the unmarried women.

Problems with feeding were relatively rare; about one of every 10 mothers (11%) described feeding as a problem. Concern about feeding usually was related to the baby either eating too slowly or too fast; some mothers felt that their baby did not eat enough.

Three-fourths of the babies were bottle fed--65% of the infants of the married women and 88% of those of the unmarried women. In about half the cases (52%) the mothers' preference was to bottle feed, a preference significantly higher among the unwed mothers. Most of the mothers preferred demand rather than scheduled feeding, and over four-fifths of the babies were being fed by demand. Only a fourth of the mothers who fed by schedule reported adhering to the schedule rigidly.

All but 7% of the infants were described as easy to manage. The usual reason given for this was that the baby ate or slept well or was a "contented baby." For the few babies described as hard to manage, the reason usually given was erratic sleeping habits or persistent crying.

A fifth of the babies were always rocked or held before going to sleep. Half were sometimes rocked or held; the rest were simply put into their bed at nap or sleep time without any preliminaries. The proportions of children being handled in these three ways by married and unmarried women were similar.

About three-fourths of the mothers (77%) said that when their babies cried during the day they might check to see whether anything was really wrong but preferred to let the baby cry and did just that. The others picked up the baby whenever she or he cried. In almost a third of these instances the mother said her preference would have been to let the baby cry, but for whatever reasons she wasn't able to do so. On the other hand, crying during the night was handled somewhat differently. Almost two-fifths (39%) of the babies were always picked up. Over half (56%) were sometimes picked up. A few mothers (5%) reported never picking up their baby despite the crying. The unwed mother was more likely to pick up a crying baby at night than was the married mother.

When asked who was more fun to care for, an infant or an older child, a fifth of the women expressed preference for an infant. About half thought an older child

Table 4-4
Most Positive and Most Negative Aspects of Motherhood

Positive	Married (N=252)	Unmarried (N=171)	Total* (N=423)
Parental role	35%	28%	32%
Companionship	23	24	23
Someone to love	19	23	21
Feeling needed	16	20	18
Other	7	5	6
Total	100	100	100

$$x^2 = 4.16, \text{ 4 d.f., N.S.}$$

Negative	(N=207)	(N=144)	(N=351)**
The work	31%	20%	26%
Loss of freedom	22	33	26
Responsibility	22	26	24
Worry	21	11	17
Other	4	10	7
Total	100	100	100

$$x^2 = 17.03, \text{ 4 d.f., p less than .01}$$

* Nine married and 16 unmarried mothers did not respond to this question

**Fifty-four married and 43 unmarried mothers did not respond to this question

more interesting. The rest thought both periods of childhood equally interesting or else said their experience was too limited to make a judgment. Only four mothers-- all married--reported at the Time 1 interview that they had no time to relax and play with their babies.

For these young mothers, the best aspects of having a baby were, in descending order, the parental role, the companionship, having someone to love, and having some- one who needs you (Table 4-4). The negatives, that is, the most difficult aspects, were the work entailed in caring for an infant, the loss of freedom, the responsibility in general of caring for someone else and the worry about the baby's well-being. Although the responses of married and unmarried women to the positive aspects of motherhood were similar, unmarried mothers were more likely to see loss of freedom as the most negative aspect. On the other hand, proportionately more married women saw the work entailed and the worry in connection with child care as negatives than was the case among the unmarried mothers.

Even for the experienced mother, caring for an infant entails at least temporary change in living pattern. About three of every five women (57%) said that they found the loss of sleep difficult and one of every three (36%) reported having problems adjusting to a loss of freedom. About a fourth (23%) of the women were finding the infant care responsibilities so time consuming that they could not carry out other responsibilities. Being unable to relax and having to adjust to a baby's demands were mentioned as difficulties by one of every 10 mothers. On each of these items the responses of married and unmarried were similar.

ASSISTANCE IN CHILD CARE

At Time 1, the majority of mothers (88%) whose babies were living with them were receiving some assistance from other persons in the general care of the child; usually--in 86% of the cases--the mother welcomed this help. When problems were reported, they generally reflected a difference of opinion between mother and helper on child care matters, or else the mother's feeling that her role was being threatened. The usual sources of assistance in baby care were the mother's parents and the baby's father. About half the women reported help from each of these sources. Over a fourth of the mothers reported assistance from other relatives, 7% said that friends were helping them, and 6% received assistance from members of the baby's father's family, neighbors or paid babysitters. Proportionately more of the unmarried women were receiving help from their parents, relatives and friends. Not unexpectedly, proportionately more of the married women were being helped by the baby's father (4) (Table 4-5).

Table 4-5

Percentage Receiving Help With Baby's Care at Time 1

Helper	Married (N=260)	Unmarried (N=182)	Total (N=442)*	x^2 (d.f.=1)	p
Parents	42	58	48	10.76	.01
Baby's father	72	16	49	127.67	.001
Other relative	20	38	28	15.59	.001
Friend	2	13	7	18.34	.001
Other	6	6	6	.91	N.S.

*Information not available on one married woman and five unmarried women

Asked about specific childcaring tasks on which they were receiving assistance (5), two-thirds or more of the mothers said they had family, friends or others who held the baby, shopped for baby items, fed and bought food for the baby. Over a third had someone helping them with the baby's laundry, and taking the baby to the doctor. Assistance in preparing the baby's food and in soothing the crying baby at night were reported by about a fourth of the women. The task on which the mothers were least likely to receive help was bathing their infant (Table 4-6).

Assistance with these early tasks of child care may enable the mother to adapt gradually to her role of motherhood. On four tasks, married mothers definitely fared better than did the unmarried women. Proportionately more of them had help with food shopping and other shopping for the baby, with taking the baby to the doctor and with soothing their crying baby during the night. Married women also tended more frequently to be helped with feeding their babies. On only one item did unmarried women receive more assistance than did married women-- help in preparing the baby's food. Although this may have been because more of these women lived with their parents, who might help with food preparation, one would have anticipated that these same women would have been receiving additional help in other areas, which was not the case.

58

Table 4-6

Percentage of Mothers Receiving Assistance With Specific
Tasks at Time 1*

Tasks	Married	Unmarried	Total	x^2(1 d.f.)	p
Holding baby	89	82	86	3.79	N.S.
Shopping for baby items	81	66	75	11.50	.001
Feeding baby	74	61	68	6.28	.05
Buying food for baby	76	58	68	14.29	.001
Baby's laundry	40	32	37	2.41	N.S.
Taking baby to doctor	43	20	34	22.98	.001
Preparing baby's food	19	32	25	7.18	.01
Soothing baby during night	32	12	24	21.13	.001
Bathing baby	19	23	20	0.87	N.S.

*Because of no responses and because items such as
preparing the baby's food were inappropriate for nurs-
ing mothers, the Ns vary: Married 197-259; Unmarried 171-181

The mothers also were asked whether they received
assistance in deciding how to handle various aspects of
child care and, if so, from whom. About four-fifths (78%)
of the women, with equal proportions of married and
unmarried, said they received such help. Usually the
married woman relied on her husband, and secondly on her
parents. The unmarried mother most always relied on her
parents, although a few got support and advice from the
baby's father.

Although about nine of every 10 mothers reported
receiving some child care assistance at the Time 1
interview, less than a third (31%) of the women anticipated
any further help in the baby's care, at least in the
foreseeable future. Anticipation of further help was true
for a much higher proportion of unmarried than married

59

women--48% versus 18%. Well over a third (36%) who expected to be helped planned on returning to work. A third (34%) planned on staying home but expected to have someone assist them with care of the baby. The rest spoke of having someone babysit as needed.

Most often it was anticipated that the woman's parents would help with the baby's care. Some expected help from other relatives and a few expected a friend, neighbor or else the baby's father to help. Three married and five unmarried women planned to hire someone.

When the mothers who anticipated no further help were asked whether they could count on anyone to take over the care of the baby if they needed to keep a doctor's appointment or the like, relatively few responded in the negative. Well over a third (37%) of the women, but only 32% of the married in contrast to 46% of the unmarried women, said they could count on more than one helper. The specific person available depended upon the marital status of the mother. Proportionately more unmarried women counted on relatives other than their parents and on friends or paid babysitters. On the other hand, proportionately more married women expected the baby's grandparents to help.

UTILIZATION OF COMMUNITY SUPPORTS AND SERVICES

In addition to the supports received by these mothers from family and friends, the study explored the availability and use of other services and supports. To what extent did the mothers find the church, the social agency, prenatal clinics and the school helpful during their pregnancy? How many of the mothers prepared themselves by attending baby care classes? What were the services perceived as needed by mothers of infants and how available were these services? Lastly, were there differences in service usage and needs depending upon the marital status of the mother?

Over half (55%) of the women in the study were Catholic. Most of the others were Protestants. A small proportion (5%) reported no religion. The distributions

60

among married and unmarried women were similar. Two-fifths of the mothers said they attended church regularly or fairly often; almost two-fifths (37%) reported attending infrequently. About a fourth (23%) of the women said they did not attend church (Table 4-7). Frequent church attendance was reported more often for the married than the unmarried women. However, only 15%--with equal proportions of married and unmarried women--reported that their church had been helpful during their pregnancy.

Table 4-7
Church Attendance

Frequency	Married (N=261)	Unmarried (N=187)	Total (N=448)
Regularly	26%	15%	21%
Fairly often	21	17	19
Infrequently	37	37	37
Never	16	31	23
Total	100	100	100

x^2 = 16.82, 3 d.f., p less than .001

One of every four women felt that both the social agency and the prenatal clinic had been of help at the time they were pregnant. About one of every 10 women said they had also been helped by the school they were then attending. Since more of the unmarried women were school-age and had used social agencies and prenatal clinics to a greater degree than had the married women, a far larger proportion of the unmarried mothers reported finding these three sources supportive.

Three-fifths of the mothers--less than half (46%) of the married but two-thirds (68%) of the unmarried women--said that at the time of hospital discharge they had been worried about caring for their baby. On the other hand, the interviewers were struck with the casual approach of a substantial number of married and unmarried mothers in

61

regard to planning for the needs and rearing of a child. That over two-fifths (43%) of the women planned to rear their children as they had been reared may indicate lack of thoughtful concern and planning, although it also could attest to a happy childhood. (Those women who did opt for different rearing usually spoke of giving their child more independence and understanding, being more consistent as parents, or in general being more responsive to their child's need for affection and attention.)

Learning more about infant needs and infant care would seem to be an obvious way of dispelling some of the apprehensions expressed by these mothers. However, despite the availability of baby care classes in most instances, a minority of women (24%) took advantage of this service before their hospital confinement. Less than half (48%) of all the mothers attended one or two classes while in the hospital.

Those attending baby care classes before their baby's birth generally attended weekly. Almost two-fifths (37%) began classes before the sixth month and only a few waited until a month or so before the "due date." Fewer unmarried women attended baby care classes either before or after delivery. However, those unmarried women who did attend started attending earlier--that is, before the sixth month.

Most (88%) of the women who attended baby care classes found that they provided needed information. However, since relatively few used this resource, only a third (34%) of all the mothers--41% of the married women but only 24% of the unmarried women--reported baby care classes as emotionally supportive during their pregnancy and infant care stage.

Over half (55%) of those not attending baby care classes said they had no need for them. Almost a fourth (23%) either did not know classes existed or else said none were easily accessible to them. About a tenth (11%) said they were too busy. A few mothers did not want to go alone; there were a few mothers who reported not taking advantage of this resource because originally they had not planned to keep the baby.

62

The most usual reason for not attending baby care classes during the hospital stay was that the hospital did not offer classes or that no classes were held during the mother's brief confinement. Some women presumably interested in attending told of classes being held at an inconvenient time; a few women reported that they were not informed about the availability of such instruction until after the class was held.

A tendency to rely on informal rather than formal supports is seen in the mothers' responses when asked who or what had been most helpful in preparing them to care for a baby. Half of the mothers mentioned a relative or friend, although about half of the time this was mentioned in combination with classes, reading, or talking with professionals such as nurses or social workers. Over a fourth (27%) alluded to their own previous experience as babysitters for a younger sibling or neighbor's child, and again about half these mothers mentioned babysitting experience in combination with classes, reading or professional help. For the rest, their knowledge usually came from reading or else from classes or professionals.

A final question to the mothers dealt with the services that they believed they needed and the availability of these services. Mothers were almost unanimous in recognizing the need for babysitters. Other services were perceived as important by far fewer mothers, with counseling the least in demand.

The supportive help needed for childrearing as seen by the married and unmarried women was not always the same, and in several instances the unmarried women expressed more need for supportive services for themselves and their babies. This was true in the case of financial help, infant day care, counseling and job training. Married women expressed more need for discussion groups on child care, a need perhaps considered a luxury by the unwed mother, with her more practical concern for daily maintenance.

On the basis of the responses, it appeared that most services perceived as needed were available to a substantial proportion of the mothers. Babysitters and persons to shop are services readily available to most of the mothers, whereas discussion groups and the opportunity of meeting other mothers are the two services least available. Differences between the married and unmarried women on perceived service availability were observable on only two items. Fewer married women saw needed financial help as being available to them. On the other hand, unmarried women tended to be less optimistic about finding better housing (Table 4-8).

Table 4-8
Percentage of 261 Married and 187 Unmarried Mothers Needing Specific Services and Percentage Having Service Available

Resources	Expressed Need		x^2	p
	Married	Unmarried		
Babysitters	98	97	0.73	N.S.
Persons to shop	27	28	0.01	N.S.
Infant day care	26	45	18.14	.001
Financial help	13	69	144.58	.001
Housing	21	26	1.25	N.S.
Discussion groups	24	15	4.62	.05
Counseling	8	22	16.80	.001
Job training	15	39	32.44	.001
Meet other mothers	30	30	0.00	N.S.

Resources	Availability if needed		x^2	p
	Married	Unmarried		
Babysitters	88	89	0.70	N.S.
Persons to shop	100	96	*	*
Infant day care	78	79	0.00	N.S.
Financial help	65	88	9.11	.001
Housing	74	49	5.73	.05
Discussion groups	38	36	0.00	N.S.
Counseling	55	75	1.62	N.S.
Job training	79	71	0.58	N.S.
Meet other mothers	49	52	0.03	N.S.

* Cells too small for x^2

INTERVIEWERS' OBSERVATIONS

After the interview, the interviewers completed a form reflecting their observations of the mothers, the condition of the home and the mother's feelings for and care of the baby. With one important exception, the ratings for both the married and unmarried women were generally positive, although significantly more so for the married women. The married women were considered to be more intelligent and to have better housekeeping standards. More of them were described as having positive feelings toward their child; fewer of the married women were described as overly casual in the care of their baby.

These ratings, made by social workers who are also mothers, are, however, impressionistic and are based on a rather limited contact. That they are more favorable for married mothers may reflect an unconscious bias. On the other hand, it is noteworthy and of some concern that the interviewers characterized the mother's feeling toward the baby as bland or rejecting for almost a fourth of these new mothers--18% of the married and 31% of the unmarried women (Table 4-9).

Table 4-9
Interviewers' Observations

	Married (N=258-261)	Unmarried (N=179-185)	x^2 (d.f.=2)	p
Condition of Home			17.15	.001
Excessively clean	15%	7%		
Average	78	76		
Dirty and disorderly	7	17		
Mother's Intellectual Functioning			17.90	.001
Above average	35	21		
Average	61	67		
Below average	4	12		

Table 4-9 (cont.)

	Married (N=258-261)	Unmarried (N=179-185)	x^2 (d.f.=2)	p
Mother's Feeling Toward Baby			12.26	.01
Extremely positive	58	44		
Positive	24	25		
Bland, rejecting	18	31		
Mother's Care of Baby			24.24	.001
Overprotective	9	5		
Average	89	82		
Overly casual	2	13		

SUMMARY

The data obtained at Time 1 revealed both differences and similarities between the married and unmarried women. The unmarried women were, on the whole, considerably younger. Fewer had completed high school and fewer had had outside employment prior to the birth of their babies. More frequently the unmarried mother lived with her parents or in other dependent living arrangements. The households in which the unmarried mothers lived were larger than the households of the married women.

The fathers of the married mothers were better educated and better off economically. Along with the apparent economic superiority of their childhood homes, the married women had fewer siblings with whom to "share the wealth." They were more likely to have been reared in intact homes and homes in which there was marital harmony, were more likely to have had the same parent figures throughout their childhood and to have had a close relationship with both their parents.

The majority of the fathers of the children were 21 years old or older, but the fathers of the children whose mothers were unmarried were considerably younger. Fewer had completed high school, more were school dropouts. Most of the men were employed; however, the fathers of children whose mothers were married were more likely to be employed in professional or technical jobs.

With rare exceptions, the fathers of children of married mothers were white, this was their first marriage, the couple had known each other at least 15 months prior to the baby's conception and the father was financially supporting the child. Although the majority of the fathers of children of the unmarried mothers were white, there was a substantial proportion who were of other racial backgrounds. Three-fourths of these men were single; usually the couple had known each other only 15 months or less prior to the baby's conception. The majority were not providing financial support for the baby; if they were supporting, the help was usually sporadic. Although most of the unmarried women had no plans to marry the father of their baby, three-fifths of them expressed a commitment to marriage, even if only for the baby's sake.

There was a substantial difference between the incomes of the married and unmarried women, with about half of the latter having monthly incomes less than $200. Yet only a third of the unmarried women felt that this was a bad time to have a baby, from the standpoint of cost. The response of the married women to this question seemed to more accurately reflect their current financial status.

Among those mothers who worked during their pregnancy, the unmarried women usually left paid employment earlier than did the married women. On the other hand, after the baby's birth, early employment was more likely for the unmarried mother, with the married mother tending to stay home with her baby. The baby of the working unmarried mother was more likely to be cared for by the maternal grandmother than was the baby of the working married woman. There were some women, both married and unmarried, who planned on working, but had not been able to arrange for child care.

About a third of the pregnancies were planned, but planned pregnancies were far less often the case among the unmarried women. Almost all the mothers knew about

67

contraceptives prior to pregnancy, but less than a third with unplanned pregnancies reported using a contraceptive device. A sizable number had relied on the rhythm method.

Some women--a higher proportion of married than unmarried--said they had not planned to become pregnant, but had no objection if it happened. About one of every six women whose pregnancy was unplanned and who had not taken measures to avoid it, reported having either no access to or information about contraceptives, a statement more frequently made by the unmarried than married women.

The majority of the women were aware of their pregnancy at an early stage and sought prenatal care from a private physician during the first trimester. Early awareness of pregnancy, early prenatal care and use of a private physician were less true for the unmarried than married women. About a third of the married women had conceived prior to marriage. About one of every seven women, more of the unmarried than married, had given some thought to aborting, and four of every 10 unmarried women had thought about adoption.

Married women were more likely to tell the baby's father first about their pregnant condition; the unmarried woman might confide in the baby's father, but also frequently used a friend as her first confidant. Emotional support during pregnancy was usually provided by a variety of formal and informal resources. Married mothers relied more heavily on the baby's father and on baby care classes than did unmarried mothers. More unmarried than married mothers received help from prenatal clinics, social workers and schools.

At the Time 1 interview most of the women described themselves as physically healthy. With the exception of feeling unable to "get going," three-fourths or more of all the mothers reported having no symptoms of psychiatric impairment.

Few of the women were members of organized groups. Preferred leisure activities most frequently were those not likely to involve interaction with others. On the other hand, most of the women reported having two or more close friends. Nearly half of the women described their neighbors as friendly and about two-fifths of the mothers visited with neighbors. Four of every 10 women, but a higher proportion of married than unmarried, attended church fairly often.

Over half the children born to these women were male. "Natural childbirth" had been desired by about three-fifths of the women, with more married women delivering by this method. Usually the birth was without complication and most of the babies returned home with their mothers shortly after birth. Most were in good health and had already been seen for a posthospital medical checkup, with the unmarried mothers using baby clinic facilities for infant medical care more than the married mothers.

Three-fifths of the mothers reported their concerns, at the time of their hospital discharge, about care of the infant. Concerns about the baby's care, finances and others' reactions to the baby's birth were more common among the unmarried women. Most women received help, and by the time of the first interview the majority reported that their worries had vanished.

A majority of the mothers expressed satisfaction with their living accommodations. The infant of the married mother most often had a room of her or his own; the infant of the unmarried mother was likely to share a room with the mother.

With rare exception the babies were described as easy to manage. Most of the children had remained in continuous care with their mother since hospital discharge. Feeding was considered a problem in about one of every 10 cases. Usually the infant was fed when she or he appeared hungry. The majority were being bottle fed, and this was more likely to be true for the infants of unmarried women.

About one of every four women attended baby care classes prior to delivery. Fewer unmarried women attended such classes. Over half the women who did not attend classes said there was no need to do so.

From the mothers' viewpoint, their relatives or friends, frequently in conjunction with classes, books, etc., were usually the most helpful resource in learning to care for a baby. Over two-fifths of the mothers planned to rear their children as they themselves had been reared, a finding that may attest to their parents' skill in child caring, but that also might be interpreted as an absence of planfulness on the part of these new mothers.

At the Time 1 interview, usually a few weeks after the mother's and baby's hospital discharge, a majority of mothers were getting some help from others in caring for their child. Parents and the baby's father were the most usual sources of help, with proportionately more unmarried women helped by parents and proportionately more married women helped by the baby's father. When questioned about help on tasks such as shopping for the baby, taking the baby to the doctor, etc., it was found that on three of nine tasks there was minimal difference between the two groups, but on five tasks married women were more likely to be helped than were the unmarried women.

At the Time 1 interview less than a third of the women--more unmarried than married--expected further help with the baby's care. But most mothers felt that they could rely on someone to "pinch hit" for them should the need arise.

Asked about resources they felt they would need in caring for their child, almost all the women mentioned babysitters. Proportionately more unmarried women expressed the need for four other resources--infant day care, financial help, counseling and job training. The majority felt that these four services would be available.

Ratings by the interviewers revealed significant differences favoring the married women and their children. The married women were considered more intelligent. Fewer were described as being bland toward or rejecting of their baby and far fewer of them were described as overly casual in the care they were providing their infant.

NOTES AND REFERENCES

1. A 1971 study of young unmarried women between 15 and 19 years old reported that among the white

women who were sexually active but did not use contraceptives, 43% were relying on the rhythm method. See Zelnik, Melvin, and Kantner, John F., "Sexuality, Contraception and Pregnancy Among Young Unwed Females in the U.S.," Demographic and Social Aspects of Population Growth, Vol. 1, Washington, D.C.: Government Printing Office, pp. 357-374.

2.   Keller, Suzanne. "The Future Status of Women in America," in Demographic and Social Aspects of Population Growth, Vol. 1. The Commission on Population Growth and The American Future Research Reports, Washington, D.C.: Government Printing Office, 1972, pp. 267-288.

3.   The preliminary data for 1974 report about 49% of all live births are female, a figure fairly constant throughout the years. U.S. Bureau of the Census Statistical Abstract of the U.S.: 1977 (98th edition) Washington, D.C.: 1977, p. 55.

4.   A separate analysis revealed that in instances in which a male partner was living with the unmarried mother, he assisted in child care matters to the same extent as did the husband of the married woman. Three-fourths or more of the men living with these married and unmarried women helped by feeding, babysitting and diaper changing. On the other hand, only a fifth of the men took responsibility for bathing the baby.

5.   The possible responses from each item were on a five-point scale ranging from no help with the task through someone else always performing the task in mother's place. This discussion, however, is concerned only with whether the mother received assistance.

CHAPTER 5
DEMOGRAPHIC CHARACTERISTICS: 18 MONTHS AND 3
YEARS LATER

A major purpose of this study was to identify those social
and behavioral characteristics, attitudes and/or experiences of the mothers that are most predictive of a positive
outcome for mother and child. This chapter describes the
mothers' living arrangements, their educational attainment,
employment and family income at Time 2, when the
children were 18 months old, and at Time 3, when they
were 3 years old.

At Time 2 relatively complete data on 241 married
and 161 unmarried mothers were obtained. Partial data
were available from returned mail questionnaires on an
additional 20 mothers, nine of whom were married and 11
of whom were unmarried at the time of their baby's birth.
The data at Time 3, when the children were approaching or
had reached their third birthday, reflect the experiences,
attitudes and opinions of 245 married mothers and of 166
unmarried women.

This chapter and the following two chapters report,
as before, those differences found at the .01 level of
significance or beyond between women who were married
and women who were unmarried at the time of the baby's
birth. Where relevant, comparable data obtained at
different time periods are presented. The reader should
keep in mind that, unless otherwise specified, references to
the unmarried women pertain to those women not married
at the time of their baby's birth.

LIVING ARRANGEMENTS, HOUSING

As at Time 1, the unmarried women at both Times 2 and 3
were more likely than the married women to live in

households in which there were no other adults present or else to live with their extended families in households in which there were several other adults and children. The home of the married mother was more typically that of the nuclear family, including both parents and one or two children.

At Time 2, about a seventh (14%) of the women lived with their parents. At Time 3 this was true for less than a tenth (8%) of the women. At both times proportionately more unmarried women than married women lived in the parental home. The proportion of married women (5%) who shared a home with their parents remained the same at both Time 2 and Time 3. However, the proportion of unmarried women sharing the home with their parents dropped from about a fourth (27%) at Time 2 to about a tenth (13%) at Time 3.

The majority (77%) of both the married and unmarried women continued to regard their housing as at least minimally adequate. Since the married women were more likely to live in the suburbs or the outer city than was the case for the unmarried women, their children more frequently had a yard in which to play. The unmarried women, who generally lived in the central city, were more likely to have easy access to stores and other community facilities.

The married women were less likely to have changed housing than were the unmarried women. At Time 3 almost half (45%) of the married women had lived in their current home 2 or more years. This was in contrast to only about a fourth (27%) of the unmarried women. Less than two-fifths of the married women (37%) had moved three or more times after the baby's birth in contrast to almost two-thirds (64%) of the unmarried women.

CHANGES IN COHABITATION PATTERNS

During this 3-year period, a variety of changes occurred in the cohabitation arrangements of almost a third (30%) of these women. Almost three-fifths (58%) of the unmarried women but only slightly more than a tenth (13%) of the married women experienced some kind of change.

74

At Time 1, 29% of the unmarried women expressed intention of marrying the putative father. By Time 3, 30% of the unmarried women had married the father of their baby; for nine of every 10 women the marriage was intact. A few others (5%) lived with the baby's father, so that at Time 3 about a third (32%) of the unmarried women were living with the father of the baby with or without the benefit of marriage. About one of every seven unmarried women (14%) had married someone other than the father of the baby; among this group a slightly lower proportion-- about six of every seven--of such marriages had remained intact. An additional 7% of the unmarried women were living with a male partner other than the father of the baby at Time 3.

Although there were a few unmarried women (2% of the total) who had lived with a male partner at some point but no longer did at Time 3, over two-fifths of the unmarried women (42%) had had no marriages nor had lived with a man throughout this 3-year period.

Among the married women, in the majority of cases (87%) the marriage was still intact. Less than a fourth of the married women who had separated from or divorced their husbands had no male partner at Time 3. Most had either entered a new marriage or were cohabiting with a male.

At Time 3, then, about half (49%) of the unmarried women but only 3% of the married women were living without the support of a husband or male partner. For the group as a whole, those living with no male support constituted slightly over a fifth (22%) (Table 5-1).

The marital or quasi-marital relationships of most of the mothers were relatively problem-free. At both Time 2 and Time 3 about nine of every 10 women who were living with a husband or male partner described their relationship as good or very good. However, at Time 2 the male partner relationship of the married women was superior to that of the unmarried women. Only 31% of the women who had not married until after their baby's birth, as compared with 61% of the women who had been married when their baby was born, described the relationship with the man with whom they were living as very good. By Time 3 the

75

Table 5-1

Changes in Cohabitation and Living Situation
at Time 3

	Married (N=247)	Unmarried (N=162)	Total (N=409)
No Change			
Remained married	87%	N.S.	53%
Remained alone	N.S.	42%	17%
Total	87	42	70
Changes, but With Husband or Male Partner at Time 3			
Was married, new husband or male partner	10	N.S.	6
Married baby's father	N.S.	27	10
Married someone else	N.S.	12	4
Living with baby's father	N.S.	5	2
Living with someone else	N.S.	7	3
Total	10	51	25
Changes, but Alone at Time 3			
Was married at time of baby's birth	3	N.S.	2
Married baby's father, now separated or divorced	N.S.	3	1
Married someone else, now separated or divorced	N.S.	2	1
Cohabited at some point	N.S.	2	1
Total	3	7	5

difference between the responses of the two groups was no
longer significant.

EDUCATIONAL ATTAINMENT OF THE MOTHERS AT TIME 3

At Time 1, over a fourth (28%) of the mothers had not
completed high school. Among the unmarried women the

proportion was markedly higher (45%). Some had dropped out of school before pregnancy. However, there were some mothers who left because of their pregnancy, most of whom intended to return to school. During this 3-year period about a fifth of the women (19%) did attend school, either full or part-time. At Time 3 a few mothers (6%) were still in school. During the 3 years following the baby's birth, more unmarried women had sought further school--29% versus 12%--but then the schooling of more unmarried than married women had been interrupted due to pregnancy.

By Time 3, four-fifths of the women had completed high school. This was the case for nine of every 10 married women (90%) and for two of every three unmarried women (67%). At the time of the third interview, a fifth of the women reported that the birth of the baby had interfered with their educational plans--13% of the married women and 29% of the unmarried women.

It is not easy for mothers to return to school after they have borne a child. Some had families who supported their endeavors; families of others were not supportive. Some resumed schooling immediately; others returned after some time. Following are case examples attesting to the strengths and resilience of some of these young women:

Anne
Anne was unmarried and a few months under 16 years of age at the time her baby was born. The baby's father is black, was just 17 and still in school. Anne dated him throughout the pregnancy but after the baby's birth they no longer were involved romantically.

Anne was described by the interviewer as "extremely naive" about sex. She knew nothing about ovulation or contraceptives and was not aware that she was pregnant until the third month. During the fourth month of her pregnancy she went to a doctor and, despite his confirmation of her pregnancy, she continued to deny it even to herself. She wanted an abortion but had no idea how to go about it. She also considered adoption but felt that both her parents and the social agency were pressuring her to surrender. This "just frustrated and upset" her.

Prior to her pregnancy Anne lived with her parents and younger siblings. She had what were described as "typical teen-age problems," feeling that her mother was "too strict and nosy." During her pregnancy she entered a maternity residence, where she completed the tenth grade.

Although supportive of Anne, her mother was concerned about assuming major care and responsiblity for Anne's baby should Anne bring the child home. Therefore, for the first 3 months the baby was placed in foster care. Anne visited him weekly, sometimes bringing him home for a few hours. The baby's father and his family also maintained contact with the baby and indicated interest in obtaining custody should Anne decide to surrender him for adoption.

After 3 months Anne's parents relented and the baby came to live with them. Anne completed high school, receiving far better grades than she had prior to her baby's birth. She also completed a year's training in a day care certification course. While she attended school her mother cared for the baby until Anne returned home, at which point Anne assumed responsibility for her baby's care.

When Anne reached 18, she and her child moved to an apartment of their own and have remained there since. Anne works full-time as a child care assistant in a day care center. Welfare assistance enabled Anne to enroll her child in a nursery school 2 days a week, and the other 3 days he attends the day care center where Anne works. Anne dates infrequently.

Although not ruling out marriage, she feels that for now it is not necessary for herself or her child. When she wants to go out at night, her mother or one of her siblings babysits for her.

Although Anne says she would have preferred to have waited until she was about 20 to have a child, since she would have been out of school and financially independent, she has found child care to be easier and less frustrating than she expected. Her son appears to be doing well and Anne is described as having much patience with him. The baby's father does not contribute to his support, but calls several times a year to find out how Anne and the baby are doing. Anne periodically takes the child to see his paternal relatives.

Anne is described by the interviewer as having become "a mature and independent young woman who is doing a fine job of rearing her son and developing herself as a person." Anne says that her child has changed her life and given her responsibilities and goals and a reason to make her life successful.

Jackie

Jackie was 16 years old, unmarried, and living with her grandmother at the time she became pregnant. Both parents had deserted the family during her early childhood. Since Jackie had run away from her grandmother's home from time to time in the past, she was placed in a foster home when it was known that she was pregnant. Following delivery, Jackie and her baby returned to this home.

Jackie, who left school when she became pregnant, had completed the ninth grade. She had known the baby's father less than 2 years, and at the time he was separated from his wife. Jackie said she had not tried to avoid pregnancy but didn't realize it was so easy to become pregnant. She considered adoption but felt that both her relatives and the social worker had put too much pressure on her to release her child.

When the baby was 6 months old, Jackie took him and moved from state to state for about a year. During this time she kept in touch with the foster mother. Eventually she returned to Milwaukee where she found an apartment for herself and her child. For a time she maintained contact with the baby's father, although he never lived with her.

During this 3-year period Jackie worked sporadically. At the Time 3 interview she was attending school part-time to get her high school equivalency diploma and working part-time at night. Like many of the mothers in this study, Jackie had had no interest in community resources. Instead she made private arrangements for someone to take her child during the week while she worked and attended school. On weekends Jackie brought the child home to live with her.

Celia

Celia was unmarried and just under 17 when her baby was born. The baby's father, a high school graduate, was black and a year older than Celia. They had known each other over 2 years but her parents disapproved of the relationship. Celia had never thought about pregnancy and knew little about contraceptives. She didn't know she was pregnant until about the fifth month, and went to the doctor for confirmation a month later.

Celia spent the last 3 months of her pregnancy in a maternity home, where she continued her schooling, but did not complete the 11th grade. She had never considered termination of the pregnancy or adoption.

After the baby's birth she returned to her parents' home and completed high school. She planned to marry the baby's father in 2 years.

80

Since her parents refused to let her bring the baby home, through social agency help he was placed in the home of a paternal aunt, and later in an agency foster home, where Celia visited him regularly. She also continued seeing the baby's father until he joined the armed services, at which point they decided to call off marriage plans. Since then, he has provided financial support for the baby and they have corresponded with each other.

When her baby was about 2, Celia found an apartment for herself and her child. Celia received minimal emotional support from her family during the 3-year period. Her mother has seen her grandchild only once and Celia's father has never seen the child. Celia is permitted to visit her parents' home, but she cannot bring the child. The social worker who supervised the child's foster care placements has continued to be supportive of Celia.

At Time 3 Celia was dating but had no plans for marriage. She is on welfare. She says that being unmarried is not a serious concern, but that if she had been older she would have had a better education, a job, more security and "nicer things." She had planned on college before the pregnancy. Her revised plan is to take child development courses and become a teacher's aide.

She is described by the interviewer as having warm, positive feelings toward her child. She says it's easier to rear a child alone than with a husband because her time isn't divided between the two. She can rear her child the way she thinks is best.

Betty

Betty was unmarried and just 20 when her baby was born. A second-year college student, she was living in a college dormitory when she became pregnant. She had known the baby's father, a 19-year-old fellow student, less than 2 years. They had planned marriage but she broke it off because she thought him a "loser." Her last contact with him was when he visited her in the hospital during her confinement. Betty did not want his support or any further ties to him.

Betty planned to surrender the child for adoption until she learned from the doctor that her condition might keep her from having another child. The baby was placed in a foster home while Betty decided what to do.

When the baby was less than 2 months of age, Betty brought him to her mother's home, where she and her baby have remained since. She returned to college and also worked part-time in the evening. Her mother and her siblings helped with the child's care, although Betty took major responsibility when she was at home.

She became active in a single-parents' group and found it helpful to discuss experiences with other members. She received financial help from welfare. Betty will be graduated from college soon, and anticipates entering a profession and becoming self-supporting.

Betty is described as ambitious and stable, with warm feelings toward her child, and solid family support. She, too, would have preferred to have been older--23 or 24--when the baby was born, so that she could have finished college and had some work experience. On the other hand, she says that now that she has had the baby for 3 years, she "can't imagine life without him."

INCOME

At Time 2 monthly income ranged from under $200 (21 mothers) to $1400 and more (10 mothers). The median income was $635. Not unexpectedly, at Time 3--a year and a half later--the median monthly income had increased to $815.

Throughout the 3 years the median family monthly income for the married women was considerably higher than that for the unmarried. At Time 2 the median monthly income for married women was $777, as compared with $355 for the unmarried. Ninety-one percent of the women who were unmarried at the time of their baby's birth, as opposed to 15% of those who were married, reported monthly incomes of under $500. At Time 3 the median monthly income for the married women was $909, but only $553 for the unmarried women.

At Time 2 about two-fifths (41%) of the women--23% of the married and 68% of the unmarried mothers--were dependent on others, most usually welfare and, less often, relatives or unemployment compensation, for income maintenance or supplementation. At Time 3 this was the case for over a third (36%) of the women. Over a fourth (27%) of the mothers were receiving welfare assistance at Time 2--only 7% of the married women but 57% of the unmarried. At Time 3 the proportion receiving welfare assistance had dropped slightly--to 23%--and at this time 9% of the married and 48% of the unmarried women were receiving some help from welfare.

Despite the relatively low incomes of these families, at Time 2 a large majority of the women (84%) said they had enough money. Not surprisingly, more of the married than unmarried women reported their income as sufficient--89% versus 76%. At Time 3 the proportion who said that they had enough money to get along was exactly the same as at Time 2. However, unlike Time 2, the difference between the proportions of married and unmarried women responding in this manner was not significant.

EMPLOYMENT

More often than not, the mothers held outside employment at least for a period after the baby was born. Only a third of the women had not worked outside the home at all. A

83

few women (5%) began working immediately after the baby's birth and continued to do so throughout the 3 years. Over a fourth (28%), although not always employed, had worked at least half or more of the time since the baby was born.

Contrary to expectations, more women were employed during the child's infancy than when the children were between 1½ and 3 years old. Whereas three-fifths of the women were in paid employment at Time 2, only about two-fifths (42%) of the women were working outside the home at Time 3. A few (4%) were looking for a job. Most of those having outside employment worked full-time during the day. A few had part-time employment; a few others held full-time jobs at night.

Usually they held clerical or sales positions; less often, they worked as waitresses, barmaids, etc. Including those working full-time and part-time, the median monthly pay for the total group was $336. The married women, who were more likely than the unmarried to be employed in part-time jobs, had a median take-home pay of $323 monthly, whereas the unmarried women's median take-home pay was $359.

Two-thirds of the employed women said they worked because they needed the money. This was true for less than three-fifths (56%) of the married women but for over three-fourths (78%) of the unmarried. Another fourth said they worked because they wanted to get out of the house, with proportionately more of the married than unmarried women working for this reason--31% versus 18%. About a tenth said they worked simply because they liked the particular job they held.

Job satisfaction appeared to be no problem for most of the women. Although the majority worked for financial reasons, over four-fifths (83%) reported that they liked their jobs. Again, this was true for more of the married than the unmarried--89% versus 75%.

Most (71%) of the women who did not have outside employment said they had no desire to work. Another 10% said they would feel guilty if they did not stay home to take care of their child. Six percent of the women said they could not find employment; a similar proportion said they did not work because the husband was opposed. A few (3%) said they wanted to work but had no one to look after their child. The others either wanted to complete their schooling first or said they were unemployed because they had no job skills.

Among those women who were unemployed and said they had no desire to work, one of three reasons usually was given for their lack of job interest. More than two-fifths (43%) believed that mothers of small children should stay home. Over a fourth (28%) said they were "too busy" with their home responsibilities. Less than a fifth (17%) said they were "happy being home."

In most instances the mother's employment was not disruptive in relation to the child's physical environment. Usually the mother employed a babysitter or else the maternal grandmother or the baby's father took responsibility for the child's care while the mother worked. In a few instances the child was cared for by other relatives, was in day care or nursery school, or was cared for by a friend. In addition to Jackie, who was described earlier, two other mothers found it necessary to arrange for their child to live elsewhere during the work week.

Gertrude

Gertrude, a high school graduate, was unmarried and 20 years old when her baby was born. Gertrude had known the baby's father over 2 years. She had used the rhythm method and had not anticipated pregnancy. The baby's father was married and although he and Gertrude continued to have daily contact throughout the 3-year period, plans for a divorce that had been discussed were never carried out. Nevertheless, he and his parents were emotionally supportive of Gertrude. He has not provided consistent financial support, but has helped out occasionally in time of need.

Gertrude first brought her baby to live with her in the apartment she had been sharing with a girlfriend. For the first few months a neighbor cared for the baby while Gertrude worked. When this plan broke down, Gertrude searched for a similar arrangement, but could not find anyone to take care of the baby while she worked. When the baby was 6 months old, Gertrude moved to her grandmother's home so that the grandmother could care for the baby while Gertrude worked.

Because Gertrude felt that she should spend most of her spare time with her baby, her social life was limited. She also wanted to live independently. Therefore, when her child was a year old, Gertrude moved into an apartment with two girlfriends. The child now lives with Gertrude's grandmother during the week and with Gertrude on weekends.

Gertrude never considered adoption and throughout the 3 years, despite layoffs from her job, she has managed to support herself and her child. She feels somewhat guilty that she is not able to have her child full-time, and is also concerned about the inconsistencies in disciplinary methods between herself and her grandmother.

As her son becomes older, she feels it is more difficult to be a mother, since there are many more decisions to be made. She also says it would have been much easier if she had had a man to help her in rearing her child. She regrets that there was not a reliable and inexpensive babysitting service that she could have used during her child's first 6 or 8 months of life, since she had such difficulty in finding a caretaker. Despite the difficulties, Gertrude says that she finds childrearing rewarding and has no regrets over having her child when she did.

Hannah

Hannah's mother died when she was about 15, at which time she was placed in a home for dependent children. After running away from that home, Hannah lived with adult friends until her pregnancy. She left school after completing the ninth grade because she "didn't like it."

Hannah was unmarried and slightly over 17 at the time of her baby's birth. During her pregnancy she lived in a foster home and, following delivery, she returned to this home with the baby. She had never worked, and planned on getting a job when she became 18.

Hannah had known the father of her baby less than a year. He was about a year older than Hannah. The pregnancy was unplanned, and the couple had used no form of contraception. After Hannah became pregnant she said she "wanted to see how it would be to have a baby."

About a year after the baby's birth, Hannah and the baby's father were married and they have been together since then. To augment the family income Hannah works. During the week the child lives with his paternal grandmother, and on weekends is home with his mother and father. Hannah wishes she had been older when she had her child--"I would have known more." However, the couple appear to be doing well and their feelings toward the child are described as warm and positive.

CHAPTER 6
THE CHILDREN'S MOTHERS AND FATHERS: 18 MONTHS AND 3 YEARS LATER

Like the preceding chapter, this chapter reports information obtained at the Time 2 and Time 3 interviews, including data on the children's fathers, the mothers' physical and emotional health, and their social supports and use of community resources. Information about additional pregnancies is also given.

THE CHILD'S FATHER OR FATHER SUBSTITUTE

In four of every five cases (81%) the biological father continued to maintain some contact with his child. Although almost all (96%) of the children of the married women had this paternal contact, this was true for only about three-fifths (58%) of the children of women who were unmarried at Time 1. Slightly less than three-fourths of the children (71%) saw their father at least weekly—90% of the children of married women but only 42% of the children of unmarried women.

In instances in which contact had been maintained between biological father and child, most (71%) of the father-child relationships were reported to be "very close." About one of every 10 fathers (9%) was reported to be indifferent or distant in relation to his child. This was far more frequently the case among the children of unmarried than married mothers—18% versus 5%. Over three-fourths (78%) of the fathers were reported to be "very pleased" to have a 3-year-old child—83% of the married versus 66% of the unmarried. On the other hand, 3% were said to be displeased, the proportions being similar among the married and unmarried groups.

89

Over half of the husbands of the married women who had become separated or divorced were giving financial support at Time 2. However, by Time 3 this figure had dropped to slightly more than two-fifths (43%). Among the unmarried women not living with the father of the child, a fourth of the biological fathers were giving regular support at Time 2. By Time 3 this was true of less than a fifth (17%).

When the total group of fathers, both those living with and those not living with the mother of the child, are considered (excluding those few cases (eight) where the father is deceased), three-fourths (75%) were providing regular financial support and an additional 4% were supporting sporadically. Sporadic or occasional support was more common among the unmarried than the married. Ninety-three percent of the women who were married at Time 1 could count on regular financial support from the father of their child, as compared with 46% of the women who had not been married.

At Time 2 two-thirds of the women who were living with husbands or male partners believed that the child's presence had improved the couple's relationship. However, at Time 3 this response was reduced to less than half (46%). Although most of the others felt that the child's presence had made no difference in the relationship, at Time 2 a tenth of the women--8% of the married but 19% of the unmarried--felt their relationship had deteriorated as a consequence of the child's presence. Nine percent of the women reported this to be the case at Time 3, but there was no difference between the proportions of married and unmarried women so reporting. When the data on all mothers who had continued their relationship with the biological father following the baby's birth were examined, it was found that over two-fifths (43%) of the women said that they had become closer to the father as a result of their child. Although a similar proportion reported no change in their relationship, there were some women (15%) who said they were less close--10% of the married women and 27% of the unmarried.

90

PHYSICAL AND EMOTIONAL HEALTH OF THE MOTHERS

As was true at Time 1, at Time 2 and at Time 3 the majority of the women described their health as either excellent or good. At Time 2, a fourth of the unmarried women, in contrast to only a tenth of the married women, said they were in "fair" or "poor" health. However, by Time 3 the proportions of married and unmarried women who described their health as "fair" or "poor" (15%) were the same.

Since the increase in drug and alcohol abuse has created considerable concern, the study attempted to explore the incidence and degree of drug and alcohol usage among the young mothers. Such questions deal with a highly sensitive area, so admittedly some responses might not accord with the facts.

As expected, alcohol was the substance the mothers most frequently reported using. Three-fifths of the women who drank said they "got high" frequently or occasionally. Although at Time 2 a substantially larger proportion of unmarried women reported this to be the case, at Time 3 no differences were found between the two groups. Few women admitted that drinking ever interfered with their ability to care for their child.

Definitions of what constituted moderate or heavy drinking and what constitutes alcohol abuse differ. Whether the women who said they drank three times a week or more fell into any of these classifications is not known. However, it is clear that between Time 2 and Time 3, there was an increase from 6% to 10% in the proportion of women who reported drinking as frequently as three times weekly or more often.

Similarly, the reported use of marijuana increased between the two time periods. Whereas less than 1% of the women admitted using marijuana at Time 2, almost a tenth (8%) said they were marijuana users at Time 3.

In addition to alcohol and marijuana, 8% of the women said they relied on barbituates on a regular or occasional basis. A few women (3%) reported using amphetamines. As clearly as could be determined, the use of these drugs was not connected with physical maladies. In the case of both barbituates and amphetamines, the proportions of users remained constant between Time 2 and Time 3. None of the mothers admitted to using heroin or LSD.

Throughout this period about nine of every 10 women described themselves as being "happy." At both Times 2 and 3, the Rosenberg Self-Esteem and the Thomas-Zander Ego Strength Scales were administered to the mothers (1). The Rosenberg scale purports to measure the self-acceptance aspect of self-esteem, while the latter test measures the individual's ability to be self-directing, to translate intentions consistently into behavior, and to control and discharge tension without disrupting other psychological processes. On both of these measures no difference was found between the married and unmarried women. Similarly, no significant difference was found between the mothers' responses at Time 2 and at Time 3.

Langner's Six-Item Psychiatric Impairment Measure (2), discussed in Chapter 3, was again administered to the mothers at both Times 2 and 3. As their children get older, do the proportions of mothers reporting specific symptoms increase, decrease, or remain the same? If change occurs, is it more likely to take place during the first 1½ years or during the later period? Do the married women continue to feel less isolated than the unmarried? If there are changes, are they more likely to be found among the women who were married at the time of their baby's birth or among those who were unmarried? Lastly, as their children get older, are the proportions of mothers reporting the various symptoms different from or similar to the proportions reported by mothers in previous studies?

For the group as a whole there was a substantial increase between Time 1 and Time 2 in the proportions reporting symptoms of restlessness, isolation and lassitude. Although the number of mothers who reported depression is small, the proportion almost doubled between Time 1 and Time 2 (Table 6-1). In general, then, it appears that these

92

Table 6-1
Psychiatric Impairment at Three Time Periods
Percentage Reporting Impairment

	Total			% Change	% Change
	Time 1 (N=448)	Time 2 (N=442)	Time 3 (N=410)	Time 1 - Time 2	Time 2 - Time 3
Restlessness	20	34	28	+14	-6
Isolation	23	34	32	+11	-2
Weakness	11	9	9	-2	0
Lassitude	45	60	54	+15	-6
Nervousness	14	22	24	+8	+2
Depression	4	7	8	+3	+1
Married at Time of Child's Birth					
	(N=261)	(N=250)	(N=245)		
Restlessness	20	33	27	+13	-6
Isolation	18	32	29	+14	-3
Weakness	11	10	9	-1	-1
Lassitude	42	58	51	+16	-7
Nervousness	12	22	22	+10	0
Depression	3	6	6	+3	0
Unmarried at Time of Child's Birth					
	(N=187)	(N=172)	(N=165)		
Restlessness	20	40	28	+20	-12
Isolation	29	43	36	+14	-7
Weakness	12	9	8	-3	-1
Lassitude	50	63	57	+13	-6
Nervousness	17	20	26	+3	+6
Depression	6	9	10	+3	+1

mothers were less well off emotionally when their children were 1½ years old than when their children were infants.

The differences between symptoms reported at Time 2 and Time 3 were much less. Although for most symptoms the proportions reporting these tended to decrease slightly or remain the same at Time 3, there was a slight increase (accounted for by the increase among the unmarried women) in those reporting nervousness and depression.

Unlike the differences found between the married and unmarried women at Time 1, at Time 2 and Time 3 no significant difference was found between married and unmarried women on any symptom. Among the women who were married at the time of the baby's birth, there was an increase of 10% or more between Time 1 and Time 2 in the proportions reporting symptoms of restlessness, isolation, lassitude and nervousness. The proportions reporting feeling depressed, while small, doubled between the first and second interview. By the time their children had reached 3 years of age, a leveling process seemed to have occurred; the proportions of married women reporting these six symptoms either decreased slightly or remained the same.

Among the women unmarried at the time of the baby's birth, the most pronounced changes are in the proportions expressing symptoms of restlessness, isolation and lassitude. By Time 3, the feeling of restlessness had subsided for a substantial number. Similarly there was a slight decrease in the proportions feeling isolated or feeling unable to get going. Depression, somewhat more of a problem for the unmarried than married mothers, increased slightly at both Time 2 and Time 3. However, the proportionate increase in depression during the first 1½ years was less for the unmarried than married women--50% versus 100%, respectively.

At Time 1, on this index of psychiatric impairment, the mothers appeared to be healthier emotionally than were the mothers in two earlier studies (3). By the time their children reached 1½ years of age, however, the differences were less marked. While significantly more of the mothers in the other studies expressed feelings of weakness and depression, differences were no longer found in the proportions who reported feeling restless, isolated, or nervous. On the other hand, whereas at Time 1 on one symptom, lassitude or an inability to get going,

94

no difference was found between mothers in this study and those in the others, at Time 2 significantly more of the mothers reported this symptom than was true for mothers in the other studies. Thus, by the time their children had reached 1½ years of age, the proportion of mothers who reported feeling restless, isolated and nervous were similar to the proportions reported by unmarried mothers whose children had reached the age of 6 and by low income mothers in New York City (4). Fewer mothers in this sample reported feeling weak or depressed, but more indicated periods of being unable to get going.

By the time the children in this study had reached the age of 3, the difference in the responses of these mothers and the Langner mothers was even smaller. Fewer mothers in this study reported feeling weak, but on each of the other five symptoms of psychiatric impairment no significant differences were found. On the other hand, the differences and similarities between this study's mothers at the Time 2 interviews and the Sauber-Corrigan mothers were maintained at the Time 3 interview. Significantly more of the unmarried mothers in the Sauber-Corrigan study reported feeling weak and depressed and significantly fewer reported lassitude.

The increase of symptoms between Time 1 and Time 2 and the decrease in differences between the mothers in this study and the mothers in the other studies suggest that childrearing, at least in its early stages, may have a negative impact on the emotional well-being of many mothers, regardless of marital or economic status. The first year and a half after the infant's birth appears to be a critical period for young mothers, after which, at least in the next year and a half, a leveling off occurs that may signify an accommodation to the mothering role. The fact that the mothers of 2-year-olds in this study differed significantly from welfare mothers on only one of the six symptoms is of special interest. Although there is no question that poverty contributes to the risk in childrearing, it may well be that the responsibility of providing infant and child care has a deleterious effect on the emotional well-being of some women, regardless of their economic status.

95

THE MOTHERS' VALUES AND CONCERNS AS PARENT AND/OR SPOUSE

The mothers were asked a series of questions concerning their role identification and role strain (5). For each activity mothers were asked to check whether they considered it very important to them, somewhat important, of little importance, or whether they preferred not to engage in the activity at all. Most women seemed to identify clearly with their role as parent and, where appropriate, as spouse. Ninety percent or more of the women attached high importance to the four activities directly concerned with their children and with their husband or male partner. Four-fifths of the mothers considered it important that they should be responsible for keeping in touch with their relatives, and three-fourths (76%) thought it important that they get family recreation started. Less than two-thirds (64%) saw their role as housekeeper as important to them, and earning an income was considered an important activity for about half (49%) of the mothers. On only two of the activities did more than 5% of the mothers express a preference not to be involved. Approximately a fifth (21%) preferred not to have to earn an income; a fairly similar proportion (18%) preferred not to have to be involved in housekeeping.

On eight questions concerning role strain, mothers were asked how frequently they worried or felt guilty about how well they performed certain activities. They could indicate whether they felt this way frequently, sometimes, or never. The responses indicated that although the majority expressed complacency, there were a significant number who were troubled by their task performance. More than a fifth (23%) said that they frequently worried about how well they taught, helped and disciplined their children. Seventeen percent reported worrying frequently about how well they cared for their children. An equal percentage expressed frequent worry about how they kept their homes (housekeeping). Earning money for the family and helping their spouse solve his problems were frequent worries for 13% of the women. Less than a tenth reported worrying frequently about how they met their spouse's sexual needs, keeping in contact with relatives and helping with family recreation.

At the other extreme, the activities on which about half or more of the women said they never felt guilty were, in descending order, helping with family recreation, earning money for the family, meeting their spouse's or male partner's sexual needs and keeping in contact with relatives. The two activities that were the least frequently reported as never being a worry were teaching, helping and disciplining their children (18%), and caring for their children (27%).

With one exception, no differences were found between the married and unmarried women with regard to their responses to these items. Forty-four percent of the unmarried women said that they never worried about housekeeping, whereas this was the case for only 28% of the married women, a difference probably accounted for by the fact that more of the unmarried women lived in the parental home and may have been relieved of this responsibility in part or totally.

SOCIAL LIFE

Despite the fact that a third of the women felt isolated, most of them maintained social contacts. Very few (1%) reported having no friends. At both Time 2 and Time 3, about three-fourths of the women said that they saw their friends at least weekly or more often. At the Time 3 interview almost all (97%) of the women reported having seen at least one friend during the previous week. For the majority of the mothers accessibility to their friends was no problem; nearly three-fifths (57%) lived within walking distance of at least one or more friends.

In addition to face-to-face contact, telephone contact with friends was also frequent. About two-thirds of the women spoke by telephone with friends several times a week; over four-fifths (82%) said they had such contact at least weekly.

The more stable housing pattern of the married women, reported earlier, is reflected in their neighborhood contacts. At Time 2, a larger proportion of married than unmarried women indicated being on friendly terms with their neighbors. Similarly, at Time 3, three-fourths of the married women visited back and forth with neighbors, in contrast to less than three-fifths of the unmarried women (74% versus 57%).

Most of the women participated in some evening social activities, relieved of the burden of child care. At Time 3, about half (48%) reported that they had an opportunity to get out at night without their child at least once a week. A fifth said they could get out about once every 2 weeks. A fourth of the women got out less often. A few women (7%) had not had any chance to get out at night without their child during the 3 months prior to the Time 3 interview.

Having a child to care for had little or no influence on church attendance. At Time 3 the mothers' reports on the frequency they attended church were similar to their reports at Time 1. Again, more of the married than unmarried women reported attending regularly--26% versus 10%. Three-fourths of the unmarried women, as compared with less than three-fifths of the married women, said they attended either infrequently or never.

On the other hand, as these women and their children have got older, there appears to be a tendency for more of the women to become involved in organized community activities such as bowling teams, arts and crafts courses, church clubs and the like. Whereas at Time 1, less than a fifth said they had engaged in such activites prior to the baby's birth, and fewer of them were then currently involved, at Time 2 almost a third (30%) had joined one or more groups. By Time 3, when the children were 3 years old, about two-fifths (38%) of the women reported being involved in group activities, most often athletics of some sort. Both at Time 2 and Time 3, these goal-oriented activities, providing opportunity for personal growth and social contact, were more frequently used by the married than the unmarried women.

98

FAMILIAL CONTACTS

For a substantial number of women there was the potential for frequent contact with parents. At Time 2, half of the women reported living within easy walking distance of their parents or just a few minutes away by car. By Time 3 this was the case for four-fifths (79%) of the mothers. Despite an increase in the number living near their parents, between Time 2 and Time 3 there was a slight decline in the frequency of contact with parents.

At Time 2 more than three-fifths (63%) of those who did not live with their parents reported seeing them at least weekly; over two-fifths (42%) saw their parents at least two or three times a week. At Time 3 the proportion of women having at least weekly contact was similar (60%), but those having more frequent contact had dropped to a third (32%).

Accessibility to and contact with other relatives was more problematic and less frequent. Data at both Time 2 and Time 3 revealed that over two-thirds of the mothers had no other relatives living nearby. Among those who did have relatives in the immediate vicinity, contact was usually frequent. The majority of these women--66% at Time 2 and 73% at Time 3--reported seeing these other relatives at least weekly. Among the married women the relatives who were most usually geographically accessible were in-laws, and, less often, siblings. Among the unmarried women the accessible relative was most likely to be a sibling and, less frequently, an in-law.

RECOURSE TO THE PROFESSIONAL FOR PROBLEM SOLVING

Between Time 2 and Time 3 there was a sharp increase in the number of mothers who sought professional help from such community resources as social agencies, psychiatrists and marriage counselors. Whereas only a fifth had sought help during the first 1½ years, almost half of the women looked to professionals for advice or counseling during the second year and a half. Throughout this period the

99

unmarried women were far more likely to seek professional help than were the married women. During the period in which the children were between 1½ and 3 years of age, three-fifths of the unmarried but less than two-fifths of the married women made use of such community resources.

A variety of community resources was used. However, the service most frequently turned to was the social agency. Help from social agencies alone or in combination with other resources was sought by a fifth of the women. Sixteen percent went to lawyers for help. A few used Planned Parenthood, a priest, rabbi or minister. Even fewer went to psychiatrists, marriage counselors or to an abortion clinic. Unmarried women used social agencies more often than did married women. Other services were used equally by both married and unmarried.

Although many of the women mentioned two or more reasons why they sought outside help, the most frequently mentioned reason--by 16% of the women--was because of family or personal problems. Next mentioned, in descending order, were health problems, financial difficulties and legal problems. At Time 3, about a fourth of the women were still seeking help.

In addition to an increase in resource utilization among the women who had never applied for help, there was an increase in the number considering using professional help. At Time 2, one of every seven women who had not sought help said that they had thought about seeking professional advice. By Time 3, one of every five women reported this to be the case. Those desiring help who had never sought it usually wanted psychiatric help and, less frequently, marital counseling or counseling for other personal problems.

A similar increase in problems or problem awareness is reflected in the mothers' response to whether they had used or considered using their community "hot-line" service. Although this service was available to most mothers, few had used it. However, whereas at Time 2 less than a third said they might, under certain circumstances, call their "hot-line," at Time 3 over two-fifths of the mothers said they might use this resource.

UTILIZATION OF OTHER COMMUNITY SERVICES

The mothers received a list of 19 services that might help them with the burdens and problems of child care and young motherhood. They were asked about both service availability and service usage. Despite the availability of several resources, the use of most was low. Two-thirds or more of the women said they had access to visiting nurse services, preschool programs, bulletins on consumer spending, parents-without-partners groups, vocational counseling, and specialized instructional programs for their children. But with the exception of bulletins on consumer spending, used by about three-fifths of the mothers, few women had taken advantage of any of these services.

Three services appealed to half or more of the mothers--swap shops for exchanging children's clothing and other children's items, organizations providing inexpensive qualified babysitting services, and supervised centers where the children could be left occasionally while the mothers attended to shopping or other errands. However, these services were available to only a tenth or less of the mothers.

In most instances, the proportions of married and unmarried women using or willing to use these 19 potential services were similar. However, more unmarried women used visiting nurses (15%). More also expressed an interest in swap shops for exchanging adult clothing and furniture (35%), special housing for mothers and children (13%), and single-parent groups (6%). On the other hand, more married women used consumer spending bulletins (65%), special instructional programs for their children (14%), and community center recreational facilities (8%).

An additional set of questions relating to other needed services or resources revealed a similar pattern of general disinterest in community services. As had been true at Time 1, at both Time 2 and Time 3 few mothers identified any of these eight unavailable services or resources as something they believed they needed. What interested the most mothers--a fifth of the women--was an opportunity to meet other new mothers. About a tenth

101

thought they might like classes or discussion groups on child care. Similar proportions expressed interest in job training and in obtaining babysitters.

Whether because of apathy, ignorance or complacency with their current situation, both at Time 2 and Time 3 the vast majority of women could not identify any other services needed that were not available to them. About one out of five did say that they could have used help when their child was younger. Usually they spoke of having needed infant day care or babysitting and, less often, discussion groups for new mothers, classes on child development and health services.

ADDITIONAL PREGNANCIES, FAMILY PLANNING AND PREFERENCES

During this 3-year period, a third of the women had given birth to a second child. A few others (1%) now had two additional children. At Time 3, one of every seven mothers was currently pregnant; an additional few thought they might be.

Further childbearing was far more common among women who had been married at the time of their baby's birth than among those who had been unmarried--44% versus 21%. In three-fifths of the cases where additional births had occurred, the pregnancy had been planned, again much more often in the case of the married than unmarried women--69% versus 34%.

In the 3-year period following the birth of their first child, a tenth of the women had miscarriages or, less frequently, abortions. The proportions of married and unmarried women were similar. However, whereas more of the unmarried women's pregnancies that terminated in this manner had been unplanned, two-thirds of the married women's were planned pregnancies.

As these women grew older, more relied on devices to prevent additional pregnancies. At Time 3 most of the women (92%) said they were sexually active--96% of the married and 86% of the unmarried. Four-fifths of the sexually active women who were capable of conception at

102

Time 3 were using some kind of birth control measure. Two-thirds relied on the pill. A fifth used either an intrauterine device or a diaphragm. Some women (6%) relied on their male partner's use of a condom; 5% used foam. A few (2%) relied on rhythm.

Despite the increased use of birth control devices, there was still a reluctance on the part of some unmarried women, in particular, to resort to them. Over three-fourths of sexually active married women who were not using birth control, in contrast to only two-fifths of the unmarried women, said that they wanted more children. The majority of sexually active unmarried women who were not protecting themselves from further pregnancies said that they did not like or believe in contraceptives.

Almost all of the women (93%), but proportionately more of the married than the unmarried, had thought about how large a family they wished to have. This ranged from "none" to "12--I love children"--both extremes being responses of unmarried women. Over half (51%) of the women who thought about the matter said they would prefer only two children. The average number desired was 2.5, a figure identical with the desired number expressed by white women between 15 and 29 years of age in 1973 (6).

REFERENCES

1. Robinson, John P., and Shaver, Phillip A. Measures of Social Psychological Attitudes, Survey Research Center, Institute for Social Research. Revised edition, 1973. University of Michigan, Ann Arbor, Michigan. pp. 81-83; pp. 132-135.

2. Langner, Thomas S., et al. "Psychiatric Impairment in Welfare and Non-Welfare Children," Welfare in Review. 7, 2 (March-April 1969), 10-21.

3. Sauber, Mignon, and Corrigan, Eileen M. The Six-Year Experience of Unwed Mothers as Parents. New York: Community Council of Greater New York, 1970.

4. Langner, et al. op. cit.

5. Nye, F. Ivan, and Gecas, Viktor. Family Analysis:
    The Washington Family Role Inventory. College of
    Agriculture Research Center, Washington State Uni-
    versity, Technical Bulletin 82, January 1976.

6. United States Department of Health, Education and
    Welfare. Advanced Data for Vital and Health
    Statistics of the National Center for Health Statis-
    tics, No. 10 Table 1. Washington, D.C., 1977.

CHAPTER 7
THE CHILDREN AND THEIR CARE: 18 MONTHS AND 3 YEARS LATER

This chapter primarily concerns the children and their care. It includes aspects of the mothers' childrearing practices, problems they experienced in caring for the children, assistance the mothers received, and interviewers' assessment of the mothers and the care they provided. The chapter concludes with a summary of the data obtained at Time 2 and Time 3.

MOTHER-CHILD SEPARATIONS

Contrary to expectations, there were relatively few disruptions in the continuity of care of the children during this 3-year period. Although detailed data were available on only 410 children, the location of 168 (93%) of the 181 children born to unmarried mothers, and 245 (95%) of the 259 children born to the married women was known. Only three children were in foster care. Two were with their maternal grandmothers, and one child lived with his father. An additional child lived part-time with his paternal grandmother because of the mother's reluctance to assume full-time care.

Only five (3%) of the 168 children of the unmarried mothers were not being cared for by the mothers. The children were being cared for either by foster parents or the maternal grandmother. All of these mothers had been 18 years old or older at the time of the baby's birth; one mother was 22. In two instances the mothers never assumed responsibility for their child. Two other children were placed in foster care before they were 1½. The fifth child began living with his maternal grandmother after his second birthday. Although some of these mothers occa-

105

sionally visit and none has taken action to surrender the child for adoption, it appears highly improbable that they will ever assume responsibility for their children.

Two of the 259 married women have abdicated their responsibility, one totally, the other partly. One mother, 16 at the time her baby was born, abandoned her husband and child after about a year. The child's father took responsibility for the child's care. The second mother, who was 20, obtained a divorce when the child was 2 years old. Although this mother was neither employed nor in school, she felt overburdened with the responsibility of caring for a child. Therefore, each week she sent the child to the paternal grandmother for several days. It appears unlikely that either of these women will assume full-time care. In both instances the child's father has been actively involved in the child's welfare and has expressed interest in taking permanent custody.

PHYSICAL DEVELOPMENT, SOCIAL ADJUSTMENT OF THE CHILDREN

Throughout this 3-year period the majority of children were in good physical health and, at least by their mothers' standards, ate well. With two exceptions--a child of a married mother and a child of an unmarried mother--no serious health problems were reported. Feeding problems of relative severity existed in fewer than one of every 10 children.

Because of the increasing recognition of hyperactivity and its potential consequences for maladaptive behavior and adjustment in young children, the study explored this area with the mothers. Reports of the children's activity level, based on the mothers' perceptions or expectations, indicated that between Time 2 and Time 3 there was an increase in the proportion considered overly active. At Time 2, less than a fifth (18%) of the children were so described; the mothers of two-fifths of these children had consulted a doctor about this. At Time 3 the proportion described as overactive had increased to about a fourth (24%).

106

Sleeping was slightly more problematic. At Time 3, the vast majority of children (96%) had their own beds. However, well over a fourth (29%) were reported to have irregular sleeping habits; about the same proportion did not sleep soundly throughout the night. Although children of unmarried women more often shared a bed with someone else, no difference was found by marital status in the proportions of children having sleeping problems.

In most instances toilet training did not begin until after the first year and a half. At Time 2, when the children were about 1½, a few (7%) were toilet trained. Among those not yet trained, over a third of the mothers (35%) were training their child; about three-fifths (59%) planned to initiate training soon. The rest had no plans at that point to begin training.

Training methods varied. About half the mothers used or planned to use rewards for bowel and bladder retention. Over a third (37%) relied on placing the child on the pot at regular intervals. About a tenth (12%) believed the best method of training included both rewards and scolding. A few mothers (2%) planned to only scold or punish the child when "accidents" occurred.

When the children were about 3 years old, all but 15% were bowel trained, usually after the child reached 2 years. Almost half (45%) were completely bladder trained. About a third (31%) had only occasional accidents, mostly at night.

Almost all of the children seen by the interviewers were regarded as average or above average in both motor development and intellectual level. In only six instances (2% of the 370 children seen at Time 3) was motor development believed to be below average. Three percent of the children were rated below average in intellectual level. Although no difference in intellectual level was found between children of married and unmarried women, children of married women were the only ones rated below average in motor development.

At age 3, peer relationships were rarely a problem among the children. All but 2% had playmates. Two children played only with their siblings. Most of the children (95%) were reported by their mothers as getting along well with other children. Three-fifths usually played with friends their own age.

CHILDREARING AND CHILD CARE

Although a substantial number of the mothers held outside employment, interest in and use of group day care facilities was the exception rather than the rule. At Time 2 only one child was in group day care. Another child had been enrolled but was removed because of the mother's displeasure with the program. At that time 6% of the mothers said they would be interested in day care within 6 months.

By the time the children were 3, 7% were in group day care. About a fifth of the women (22%) were then interested in obtaining day care immediately or within the next 6 months. However, most mothers (71%) indicated no interest in community day care.

Most of the mothers had given some thought to childrearing prior to the birth, but one of every 10 said they had had no specific ideas about how a child should be reared (7% of the married women and 15% of the unmarried women). Although almost three-fourths (73%) of the women said they read articles or books on child development and childrearing and in most instances reported such reading as helpful, more formal methods for education were used far less often. At both Times 2 and 3 seven of every eight women said that child development classes were available in the community, but few women-- less than 10%--had attended such classes.

Even though a majority of the mothers had sought child care information through reading, the proportion of women (43%) who said they were rearing their child as they had been reared remained the same as at Time 1. Half of the married women, but only a third of the unmarried, reported using their parents as models.

About two-thirds of the mothers admitted that their earlier perceptions relative to behavior management had not been realistic. Most found childrearing more difficult than anticipated. A substantial proportion (22%) reported that their experiences had made them aware that they had to lower their expectations of perfect behavior, instant obedience, etc. Others (13%) said they realized that a child required more discipline than they had expected. In only one instance was a difference found by marital status. Although over a fourth (29%) of the married mothers spoke of lessening of expectations, this was true for only about an eighth (13%) of the unmarried women.

The reports of these women indicate that between infancy and 1½ years, as the mothers became more accustomed to childrearing, they found their role easier. However, during the second year and a half, as the child became more mobile, more of the mothers found child care more difficult. At the time the children were a year and a half old, three-fifths (61%) of the mothers said they found child care easier than when the child was an infant. Less than a third (30%) reported that the care of a 1½-year-old child was harder than the care of an infant. The rest saw no difference in responsibility in the two periods. By the time the children had reached their third year, only half (52%) of the mothers regarded childrearing as easier than at an earlier period. Almost two-fifths (38%) reported that they found it harder. Again, a minority (10%) saw no period as different from another.

For most mothers, the difficulties of child care were unrelated to the personal satisfaction obtained in mothering. Although childrearing had become admittedly more difficult for about two-fifths of the women, a majority (88%) said childrearing was more rewarding than anticipated. Four-fifths of the mothers (79%) reported receiving more pleasure from their 3-year-old child than from their child as an infant. Only a fifth (19%) reported that the infant period was more pleasurable for them.

Though some mothers reported increasing difficulty as the child became older and more active, most regarded the responsibility of child care as very easy or moderately easy. At Time 3 a fifth of the women found it moderately hard (18%) or very hard (2%). Those finding it hard usually spoke of "behavior problems" or of feeling overburdened or inadequate. A few (7%) said they simply did not like the role of parent. Despite their admission of problems, only a small proportion (5%) said they frequently wished they did not have the burden of a child. Most mothers (90%) said that this was an occasional wish on their part.

Discipline was an area of concern for most mothers (97%). Over a fourth (27%) admitted that they frequently became impatient with the child. About two-thirds (65%) admitted to being impatient occasionally. Only a few (8%) said that they rarely were impatient.

The mothers usually relied on one or more of four types of disciplinary measure. About a third said they usually scolded or talked to the child; an equal proportion said they resorted to spanking or sending the child to her or his room. The rest generally used all four types of discipline. The mothers varied in their beliefs about the most effective punishment. Spanking or slapping, reasoning, and isolation were the punishments most frequently mentioned. About a tenth of the women reported scolding to be most effective. Smaller proportions considered either deprivation of privileges or withdrawal of love from the 3-year-old child as the most effective. Fewer still (3%) said "nothing" worked effectively.

During the 2 weeks preceding the Time 3 interview, a third of the children had received six or more spankings. A third had been spanked only once or twice; almost a tenth (8%) had not been spanked at all. In most instances the child was spanked on the buttocks or limbs, but about a tenth (9%) of the mothers reported hitting or slapping the child's face or head. Although some mothers (15%) reported using such objects as paddles, straps, ropes and wooden spoons, the majority said that they used only their hands when administering physical punishment. The mothers' views of the effectiveness of spankings were divided fairly evenly among four categories. Over a fourth (27%) had no reservations about the positive value of spankings. Others (29%) thought they did some good, but had some reservations. A fifth of the women had mixed feelings about this type of punishment. The other fourth believed that spankings were ineffective.

110

As to the mothers' attitude and consistency in discipline, about half (46%) reported that they always followed through on threats. About a third said they sometimes did not follow through. Over a fifth (22%) admitted that although they threatened their child with punishment, they frequently did nothing about it, though the misbehavior continued.

Among parental restraints in day-to-day living, it was found that the greatest latitude for the child was related to watching television, listening to the radio, records, etc. Almost half (45%) of the mothers said they placed no restrictions on these activities. About one of every six mothers (16%) said the child went to bed at night whenever she or he wished. An equal proportion imposed no restrictions on noise the child could make in the home.

Not surprisingly, in view of the age of the children, the activity on which the mothers imposed the most restrictions and exercised the greatest caution related to the child's whereabouts when playing outdoors. Almost three-fourths of the mothers (73%) restricted the child to the yard. About three-fifths (58%) frequently or always checked when the child was not within sight. Very few mothers (1%) said they had no restrictions on where their child might play outside. Few (4%) said they almost never checked on the child's whereabouts.

Three other aspects of child care management on which a tenth or more of the women indicated that they were strict were table manners (15%), respect for furniture, walls and other objects in the home (13%), and bedtime rules (10%). However, on these and other matters, most mothers did not expect immediate conformity. Three-fourths said that although they wanted and expected obedience, they usually anticipated that the child would require several commands before acceding. A minority (24%) indicated that they expected conformity immediately or certainly after they spoke to the child twice. Very few mothers (1%) said they did not expect a 3-year-old child to obey at all.

By the time the children were 3, almost all were being taught some table manners, how to dress and wash themselves, how to brush their teeth, and to discriminate among colors. About nine of every 10 children (87%) had commenced learning letters of the alphabet, simple numbers, or drawing. Over four-fifths of the mothers read to their child daily or upon request. Few mothers (4%) said they never read to the child.

CHILD CARE ASSISTANCE

Although in many instances the mothers relied on relatives for help in child care matters, neighbors were also a source of help for some. At Time 2 over two-fifths (42%) of the married women, but less than a third of the unmarried women (29%), said that neighbors had helped out by babysitting. By Time 3 almost half (49%) of the married but only about a third (32%) of the unmarried women were receiving such child care assistance from neighbors.

At Time 3, it was easy for the majority (86%) to find someone to care for the child if they had to go out. If they wanted to go out at night, over two-thirds (68%) said, they could rely on relatives. About two-fifths (39%) used paid babysitters on occasion, although usually these mothers relied on relatives, neighbors or friends to babysit.

Most mothers (85%) received some help with the child's care, other than what was necessary for those who were employed or attending school. Almost two-fifths (37%) received such help less often than weekly. Over a fourth (28%) said that others helped with child care from two to six times a week. Nearly a fifth (17%) had help on a weekly basis. A small number of mothers (3%) reported that someone helped them daily. The maternal grandmother was usually the person who helped with the child's care.

Questions similar to those addressed to the mothers at Time 1 were asked again at Time 3. These questions related to the help that the mothers received with specific childcare tasks, and were asked of all mothers who had either full- or part-time responsibility for their child's care. From two-thirds to more than nine-tenths of the mothers had help with six of the nine tasks asked about.

112

They were least likely to have help with bathing the child, toilet training and taking the child to the doctor. For several tasks the married women were more likely than the unmarried women to have some assistance. This was true in the case of help with dressing the child, deciding about their child's activities, discipline, bathing and putting the child to bed for naps and at night. Unlike Time 1, in no instance did unmarried mothers receive more assistance than married women (Table 7-1).

Table 7-1
Percentage of Mothers Receiving Assistance
With Specific Tasks at Time 3

Tasks	Married (N=244)	Unmarried (N=163)	Total (N=407)	x^2 (1 d.f.)	p
Dressing child	84	69	78	11.49	.001
Getting child's meals	68	68	68	0.00	N.S.
Deciding about child's activities	95	78	88	26.06	.001
Discipline	95	88	92	7.29	.01
Bathing	64	45	57	13.52	.001
Putting to bed	82	60	73	21.69	.001
Toilet training	56	44	51	4.97	.05
Taking child outdoors	93	87	91	4.76	.05
Taking child to doctor	34	25	37	4.05	.05

Most mothers received emotional support in their child care role. This was more often true for the married women. Indeed, during the second year and a half there was a diminution of such support among unmarried mothers.

At both Times 2 and 3, the mothers were asked to whom they turned for help when problems arose with regard to their child. A small proportion of the married women--3% at Time 2 and 2% at Time 3--said there was no one to whom they turned. Six percent of the unmarried mothers at Time 2 and 9% at Time 3 gave this answer.

Not only did the source of emotional support differ by marital status, but it changed over time. At Time 2, the persons mentioned most frequently by the married women were their mothers (38%) or their husbands (32%). Over a tenth of the married women (13%) at Time 2 said they usually turned to friends and 11% said they turned to other relatives. By Time 3, the maternal grandmother was used much less frequently by the married women than had been the case at Time 2. About a fourth of the married women said they turned to their mothers when they needed advice or help; half (51%) said they always turned to their husbands or boyfriends.

The child's grandmother most frequently provided this kind of emotional support for the unmarried women at Time 2 but to a lesser extent at Time 3. At Time 2, over half (55%) of the unmarried women said that they turned to their mothers for help. At Time 3, a third of the women mentioned their mother as a source of emotional support. Husbands or male partners were mentioned by about a tenth of the originally unmarried women at Time 2 but by about a fourth of the unmarried women at Time 3. At both Times 2 and 3 the unmarried women used friends and other relatives in about the same proportions as did the married women.

OTHER ATTITUDES, THE INTERVIEWERS' RATINGS

At Time 1 a question addressed only to the unmarried women revealed that almost two-fifths (38%) of them believed that being single was no handicap to motherhood. At Time 2, when both the married and unmarried women were asked whether they believed childrearing was easier alone or with a man to help, over a third (35%) of the unmarried women maintained either that it was easier alone or that it made no difference. A year and a half later, when the children were 3 years old, the proportion responding in this manner had dropped to 28%.

A similar response was made by only 9% of the married women at Time 2 and by an even smaller proportion (6%) at Time 3. The usual reasons given by both the married and unmarried women who denied the importance of a male partner in childrearing were, in descending order: it is better to have only one decision maker; a man "doesn't help anyway" or "others can help just as well"; rearing a small child is "a woman's job." Those women who believed childrearing to be easier with a man to help usually spoke of the man's supportive role in the family. A fairly substantial number saw his importance as a disciplinarian--"a child listens to a man more." A few mentioned help with childrearing tasks and others saw him providing a "male image" for the child.

Since many of these women had been extremely young when they gave birth, and since they now had 3 years' experience with both the negative and positive aspects of motherhood, the mothers were asked how they felt about having their first child when they did. Half (52%) said they were satisfied with the timing of the first child. This was true for three-fifths (61%) of the married women, and two-fifths (39%) of the unmarried women. Very few (1%) said they would have preferred having their first child when they were younger, whereas over two-fifths--substantially more of the unmarried than married women--said they would have preferred to wait until they were older. The remaining women--2% of the married and 5% of the unmarried--said they would rather not have had a child at all (Table 7-2).

Table 7-2
Preferred Timing and Mother's Marital Status

Preferred Timing	Married (N=245)	Unmarried (N=165)	Total (N=410)
As it was	61%	39%	52%
When older, younger	37	56	45
Never	2	5	3

$$x^2 = 19.38,\ 2\ d.f.,\ p\ \text{less than}\ .001$$

When the data were controlled by marital status with the mother's age at the time of her baby's birth, no difference was found by age in the preferences of married and unmarried women. However, the mother's age in and of itself is significantly related to her response and accounts for the difference found by marital status. The older the mother at the time she gave birth, the more likely she was to say that she was satisfied with the timing (Table 7-3).

Table 7-3
Preferred Timing and Mother's Age at Baby's Birth

Preferred Timing	Under 20 (N=169)	20-22 (N=148)	23 and above (N=93)
As it was	31%	60%	77%
When older, younger*	64	37	22
Never	5	3	1

$$x^2 = 55.06, \ 4 \ \text{d.f.}, \ p \ \text{less than} \ .001$$

*Only 1% of the respondents, all 20 years of age or older, said "when younger."

Whereas at Time 1, 76% of the mothers were rated by the interviewers as having warm or positive feelings for their child, at Time 2, 85% were so rated. The remaining women were judged as bland, ambivalent or rejecting. At Time 3 the percentage described as warm or positive had dropped back to 73. Neither at Time 2 nor Time 3 were significant differences found between the attitudes of the married and unmarried women.

At Time 2, with rare exceptions, the mothers were believed to take a positive interest in their child's development. However, at Time 3 a tenth of the mothers were rated as appearing uninterested in their child's development and offering the child little or no stimulation. At Time 3 in 4% of all the cases, interviewers expressed concern about the potential for neglect or abuse of the child, but in no instance was there sufficient evidence to verify neglect or abuse.

116

SUMMARY

The last three chapters have presented data obtained from the mothers when their children were 1½ years old and again when their children were about 3. In several instances data obtained at two and sometimes three points in time could be compared.

The original study group had consisted of 448 children. Five children (3%) of the unmarried mothers were permanently surrendered within the child's first year, and two married mothers and one unmarried mother died. At the 3-year interview the whereabouts of 413 (94%) of the remaining study group were ascertained.

Contrary to expectations, relatively few children had experienced a disruption in the continuity of care and, with rare exceptions, the children were still being cared for by their biological mothers.

Generally the health of both mother and child was reported good. Most of the children were bowel trained, had regular sleeping habits, and were said to get along well with other children.

Forty-four percent of the mothers unmarried at the time of their child's birth married during the 3-year period. At Time 3 about half of the initially unmarried group and almost all (97%) of the married group were living with a husband or male partner. Housing for most (77%) of the mothers was considered to be at least minimally adequate, and more than 80% reported income sufficient for their needs. Nine of every 10 women who were living in a marital or quasi-marital relationship considered this relationship good.

Almost nine of every 10 women (88%) said that they had found childrearing more rewarding than anticipated. But about half the mothers would have preferred to have waited until they were older before having a child, the younger mothers expressing this preference far more often than the older mothers.

On Langner's Six-Item Psychiatric Impairment measure, a substantial increase was found in symptoms reported by the mothers at the time their children were 1½ years than when they were infants. In most instances the

117

symptoms seemed to have subsided or leveled off by the time the children reached 3, but at that point it was found that the proportions of mothers reporting symptoms of psychiatric impairment were similar to the proportions of low income mothers reporting such symptoms in an earlier study. These findings suggest not only that the early childrearing period--between birth and 1½ years--is a critical period for mothers, but that mothering itself is stressful, regardless of income or financial supports.

Discipline loomed high in the mothers' problems. Although few expressed a need for services that might be helpful, a fifth said they would like to share experiences and concerns in coping with their problems. A peer self-help group might have been acceptable to and facilitative for many of these mothers.

Between Time 2 and Time 3 there was a large increase in use of formal community resources such as social agencies, lawyers and public health nurses. Whereas only a fifth of the mothers used such resources during the first year and a half after giving birth, about half the mothers did so during the second year and a half. Social agencies were the most frequently used resource, but the percentage of women who had recourse to lawyers was only slightly less--29% and 16%, respectively. There was also a slight increase between Time 2 and Time 3 in the percentages of mothers who said they desired professional help but did not seek it--from 14% at Time 2 to 20% at Time 3. The increase in help sought or desired suggests an increase of problems.

An increase in stress, as childrearing progresses, is suggested in the responses of the unmarried women to the question of whether it is easier to rear a child alone or with the help of a man. At the first interview 38% of the mothers saw their single state as no hardship, at Time 2, 35%, and by Time 3, only 28%.

Additionally, between Time 2 and Time 3 there was a slight decrease--from 61% to 52%--in the percentage of mothers who found childrearing easier than they had earlier.

118

In many instances no differences were found between women who were married at the time of their baby's birth and those who were unmarried. But more of the unmarried women, being younger, continued schooling during the 3-year period.

Financially, the unmarried mother and her child were in more jeopardy. Far more unmarried than married women had to rely on welfare. More unmarried women worked full time rather than part time, and more of them were working because they needed the money. Among the married women, work was more frequently used as an opportunity to get out of the house. More married than unmarried liked their jobs.

The married woman was likely to have more informal supports than the unmarried woman; more likely to have someone to turn to if she had problems with her child; and more likely to be helped by neighbors. She was also more likely to be involved in organized social activities in her community. The unmarried mother, with fewer informal supports, was far more likely to use formal community resources.

CHAPTER 8
VARIABLES ASSOCIATED WITH ADJUSTMENT

This chapter presents those variables found to be associated with the mothers' and children's adjustment. Contrary to expectations, marital status, age and socioeconomic status proved relatively insignificant factors on most measures of adjustment. The factors most closely related to the mother's adjustment were personality variables such as psychiatric impairment, attitude toward pregnancy, and permissiveness with regard to her child. The three factors most closely related to the child's adjustment were the degree of the mother's contentment, the mother's use of corporal punishment, and the child's physical health.

I. VARIABLES ASSOCIATED WITH THE MOTHER'S ADJUSTMENT

Six measures of adjustment were developed. This section presents these measures in the order of the degree of variance accounted for, and identifies the variables that accounted for a significant proportion of variance in each.

A. Mother's Contentment at Time 3

This index was developed as a measurement of the mother's general sense of well-being and contentment with her role as parent, at the time her child was 3 years old. The index included the mother's responses to three questions on satisfaction with her maternal role, and her scores on the Rosenberg Self-Esteem and Thomas-Zander Ego Strength Scales. In addition, the index included an assessment by the interviewer of the mother's feelings toward her child.

121

At one end of this scale are mothers who described themselves as very happy. They scored high on self-esteem and on ego-strength. They were glad they had their child when they did, found childrearing more rewarding than they anticipated, and were described by the interviewer as warm and positive toward the child.

Mothers scoring low described themselves as unhappy, having low self-esteem and low ego-strength. They would have preferred having the child later or not at all. They found childrearing less rewarding than anticipated and were described by the interviewer as being rejecting, ambivalent or bland toward the child.

Five variables accounted for 50% of the variance in the mother's contentment scores. These were psychiatric impairment, permissiveness in childrearing, use of community resources to help in parenting, her perception of unavailable resources needed, and her attitude toward pregnancy as reported in the first interview.

1. Psychiatric Impairment

The strongest factor, accounting for 40% of the variance in the mothers' contentment scores at Time 3, was psychiatric impairment. As mentioned earlier, the psychiatric impairment index was developed by Langner and consists of six items used to measure the mother's disability. These items describe whether the mother feels weak, restless and isolated, and the frequency with which she experiences "feeling nervous," being in poor spirits, or being "unable to get going." Mothers scoring high on impairment were likely to have reported several, though rarely all, of these symptoms.

Three-fifths of the mothers who scored low in psychiatric impairment were found to be highly contented, in contrast to about a fourth of the women moderately impaired and a tenth of the mothers highly impaired. Although the relationship between impairment and contentment is linear, not all mothers who scored high in impairment were highly discontented, nor were all mothers with low psychiatric impairment either highly or moderately contented (Table 8-1).

122

Table 8-1
Mother's Contentment at Time 3
and Psychiatric Impairment

Degree of Contentment	Degree of Psychiatric Impairment		
	Low (N=143)	Moderate (N=123)	High (N=144)
High	59%	27%	10%
Moderate	31	48	38
Low	10	25	52

$$x^2 = 104.84, \text{ 4 d.f., p less than .001}$$

2. Parental Permissiveness

Some parents set high standards for their children, others demand little. Are children and parents at one end of the continuum any better off than those at the other? Or is a position midway or at some other point between permissiveness and strictness more conducive to the well-being of parent and child?

To examine these questions, an index of parental permissiveness was developed. At one end of the scale were mothers who placed no restrictions on how their children treated furniture, walls and other objects in the home. These mothers had low standards regarding neatness, permitted their children to go to bed when they pleased, allowed unlimited use of the television and radio, had no expectations of obedience from their children and seldom if ever followed through on threats. At the other end were those mothers who would be regarded as extremely strict.

The permissiveness variable accounted for 4% of the variance in the mothers' contentment scores. Mothers who were the most contented were the least permissive. Although over two-fifths of the mothers who were low on permissiveness--placed high restrictions on their children-- were highly contented, this was the case for less than a third of the mothers who were moderately strict and for only a fifth of the mothers who placed few restrictions on their children (Table 8-2).

123

Table 8-2
Contentment at Time 3 and Parental Permissiveness

| | Parental Permissiveness | | |
| | High | Moderate | Low |
Degree of Contentment	(N=114)	(N=154)	(N=140)
High	19%	31%	45%
Moderate	37	42	35
Low	44	27	20

x^2 = 26.77, 4 d.f., p less than .001

3. Use of Community Resources

Earlier the pervasive disinterest of these mothers in using community resources was noted. A question of interest is whether mothers who use such resources are better off or worse off than mothers who do not. An index reflecting use of community resources during the early childrearing period was developed. The items primarily· pertained to attendance at groups or classes that might enhance the development of mother and child. Responses to questions concerning the mother's use of books or articles about child care or child development, as well as materials that help her as a homemaker, were also included.

Table 8-3
Contentment at Time 3 and Resource Utilization

| | Number of Resources Used | | | |
| Degree of | None | One | Two | Three,More |
Contentment	(N=93)	(N=133)	(N=131)	(N=53)
High	19%	25%	39%	57%
Moderate	49	34	37	36
Low	32	41	24	7

x^2 = 37.14, 6 d.f., p less than .001

124

As can be seen in Table 8-3, the more resources the mother used, the more contented she was at Time 3. Almost three-fifths of the mothers who used three or more resources were high in contentment. This was the case for about two-fifths of the mothers who used two resources and for fewer of those mothers who used one resource or none. Only 7% of the mothers in the low contentment category used three or more resources.

4. Resource Needs

At each of the three time periods the mothers received a list of community resources, ranging from specific services such as babysitters, to counseling or problem sharing with other mothers. They were asked whether each of these resources was available to them. For resources not available, they were asked whether they would be useful. Seven items were included in the Time 3 index.

The lower the number of needs, the higher contentment of the mother. The number of unavailable community resources perceived by the mother as either desirable or crucial at Time 3 accounted for 3% of the variance in mother contentment scores. Only a fourth of the mothers who identified three or more community supports as needed but unavailable were in the high contentment category. This was true for a third of the mothers who named one or two needs. Among those reporting no unmet needs, two-fifths were highly contented (Table 8-4).

Table 8-4
Contentment at Time 3 and Resource Needs

Degree of Contentment	Number of Needs		
	None (N=106)	One, Two (N=149)	Three, More (N=154)
High	41%	33%	26%
Moderate	39	40	36
Low	20	27	38

$$x^2 = 11.97, \text{ 4 d.f., } p \text{ less than } .05$$

5. Attitude Toward Pregnancy

It was predicted that the mother's attitude toward the pregnancy and the advent of a baby into her life would be associated with the mother's and child's later adjustment. This attitudinal measure consisted of nine items. The data were obtained from the mother shortly after her baby's birth.

Attitude toward pregnancy was found to be significantly related to contentment score at Time 3. As shown in Table 8-5, more of the mothers who reported positive attitudes toward pregnancy and the prospect of having a baby were in the high contentment category--44% as compared with 27% of the ambivalent mothers and 23% of the mothers with negative attitudes. Although more mothers with positive attitudes scored high and fewer scored low in contentment, differences between mothers whose attitudes were ambivalent or negative were minimal.

Table 8-5
Contentment at Time 3 and Attitude Toward Pregnancy

Degree of Contentment	Attitude Toward Pregnancy		
	Positive (N=164)	Ambivalent (N=113)	Negative (N=133)
High	44%	27%	23%
Moderate	36	35	44
Low	20	38	33

$$x^2 = 21.77, \text{ 4 d.f., p less than .001}$$

B. Mother's Contentment at Time 2

This index measured the mother's general sense of well-being when the child was 1½ years old. Except for the ego strength scale and the interviewer's assessment, it consisted of items similar to those in the Time 3 index. Mothers who scored high in contentment had good self-esteem and not only described themselves as happy, but

126

considered themselves happier than they were before their baby's birth.

Five variables accounted for 40% of the variance in the mother's contentment with herself and her role as parent at the time the child was 1½. These were her degree of psychiatric impairment, her coping capacity, the number of resources she needed, the pleasure she received from mothering, and the presence or absence of the baby's father or a husband in the home.

1. Psychiatric Impairment

As with the contentment scores at Time 3, the strongest of the relationships, accounting for 28% of the variance when the children were 18 months old, was the mother's psychiatric impairment. Again, the relationship was linear. Almost half of the mothers relatively unimpaired scored high in contentment; only a fifth of the moderately impaired women and less than a tenth of those highly impaired were in the high contentment category. (p less than .001)

2. Mother's Coping Capacity

Responses to the 27-item Thomas-Zander Ego Strength Scale were used to measure coping capacity at Time 2. Mothers scoring high were generally self-directing, and could deal appropriately with internal tension. Coping capacity accounted for 8% of the variance in contentment scores. The greater her coping capacity, the more likely a high score on contentment.

As shown in Table 8-6, half of the mothers who had high coping capacity were highly contented, in contrast to a fifth of those who had moderate coping capacity and only 5% of those in the low capacity category.

3. Resource Needs

As had been found in the case of the mother's contentment at Time 3, the number of community

Table 8-6
Contentment at Time 2 and Coping Capacity

| | Mother's Coping Capacity | | |
Contentment	Low (N=118)	Moderate (N=199)	High (N=105)
High	5%	21%	50%
Moderate	60	63	43
Low	35	16	7

$$x^2 = 79.05, \ 4 \ d.f., \ p \ less \ than \ .001$$

resources perceived as needed but not available also was significant, accounting for 2% of the variance in contentment scores at Time 2. Almost a third of the mothers reporting no unmet needs scored high in contentment, in contrast to a fifth of those with one or two unmet needs and only 13% of those who mentioned three or more. A third of the women with three or more unmet needs were in the low contentment category. This is in contrast to less than a fifth of the other mothers. (p less than .001)

4. Pleasure in Mothering an Infant

Mothers vary in preferences and in degree of pleasure they receive from their children at various stages. Some prefer infancy; others do not feel strong gratification until the child is older. The 66 mothers who scored low on this variable were in the latter group. They had not found infant care pleasurable and their feelings were ambivalent at best.

This variable accounted for some of the variance in the mother contentment scores at Time 2. Mothers who took considerable pleasure in infant care were more likely to be highly contented than mothers who received little or no pleasure from caring for an infant (Table 8-7).

5. Presence of a Husband or Male Partner

The fifth variable was whether a husband or male partner was present in the home. Mothers without this source of support at Time 2 were far more likely to be low

Table 8-7
Contentment at Time 2 and Pleasure in Mothering an Infant

	Pleasure in Mothering		
	High	Moderate	Low
Contentment	(N=121)	(N=230)	(N=66)
High	31%	22%	15%
Moderate	55	59	56
Low	14	19	29

x^2 = 10.27, 4 d.f., p less than .05

Table 8-8
Contentment at Time 2 and Presence of Husband or Male Partner

	Husband/Male Partner in Home	
	Yes	No
Contentment	(N=296)	(N=126)
High	27%	16%
Moderate	59	52
Low	14	32

x^2 = 20.08, 2 d.f., p less than .001

in contentment than mothers who did have this support (Table 8-8).

C. Success Over Time

A summary score was developed that included the mother's contentment scores at Times 2 and 3, as well as her ease in caring for her child at these two time periods. Scores based on the interviewers' assessments at Time 1 through Time 3 of the mothers' feelings for, interest in and care of their children were also included. The intercorrelation of these five measures were all significant at the .001 level, ranging from .20 to .52.

At one end of the scale were those mothers who found child care very easy and were very contented. They were likely to receive a high rating from the interviewers at each time period with regard to feelings for, interest in, and care of the child. At the other extreme were mothers who found child care difficult. They may have been discontented with themselves and with their parenting role, and were likely to have been rated by interviewers as less warm toward their child, perhaps providing little stimulation, care and protection and, in some instances, raising a question of neglect.

A review of the data revealed that although a mother might rank very high on two or three measures, she was likely to rank moderately high on the other measures. In no instance did a mother rank very high or very low on all of the measures used in this index of success. Thus, no mother could be considered an outstanding success or complete failure.

About 17% of the scores fell at either end of the measure. Twenty-six percent of the mothers were in the middle range and the rest were between the middle and the extremes.

When the data were entered into a multiple regression, two maternal characteristics and five other variables dealing with attitudes, behaviors and resource needs were found to be significant and to account for 35% of the variance in the success scores. These were the mother's psychiatric impairment, permissiveness, use of corporal punishment, resource needs, health, resource utilization, and attitude toward her pregnancy.

1. Psychiatric Impairment

The first variable, contributing 12% of the variance, was the degree that the mother was impaired at Time 1. Psychiatric impairment during the very early child care phase was clearly related to her score on the overall measurement of success. Over half of the low impairment mothers were high scorers, as compared with slightly over a third of the moderately impaired and a fifth of the highly

130

impaired mothers. Among the low scoring mothers the distributions of low, moderate and high impairment mothers are almost identical in reverse. (p less than .001)

2. Permissiveness

An additional 8% of the variance in the scores was attributed to the mother's permissiveness. The relationship was linear and it was similar to the relationship between the mother's contentment at Time 3 and permissiveness. The less permissive the mother, the more likely that she scored high on overall success. (p less than .001)

3. Corporal Punishment

Disciplinary techniques varied, of course, among mothers, many relying on scoldings and other verbal forms of punishment, others relying more on spankings or slaps. Were differences in outcomes for mother and child associated with the degree of physical punishment?

Five items reflecting the mother's use of such punishments were combined into an index. Mothers scored high who had spanked their children frequently during the 2 weeks preceding the Time 3 interview. They frequently resorted to a strap, stick or paddle. They also reported slapping their children, sometimes on the face or head. They said they found physical punishment effective.

The variable on corporal punishment contributed 5% to the variance in the success scores. As shown in Table 8-9, the association between corporal punishment and overall success was linear. Half of the mothers who used corporal punishment rarely or never had high success scores, as opposed to about two-fifths of those who used corporal punishment moderately and to only a fourth who used corporal punishment extensively.

4. Resource Needs

The variable of perceived need for community resources unavailable to the mother at Time 2 contributed

131

Table 8-9
Success and Use of Corporal Punishment

| | Use of Corporal Punishment | | |
| | Low (N=118) | Moderate (N=157) | High (N=112) |
Success			
Very high	25%	15%	10%
High	25	22	13
Moderate	25	28	25
Low	18	17	29
Very low	7	18	23

$$x^2 = 27.06, \text{ 8 d.f., p less than .001}$$

4% to the variance in the success scores. The relationship was linear. Almost half of the mothers reporting no unmet needs scored high, in contrast to about two-fifths of those with one or two needs and only a fourth of those who said they needed three or more services. Conversely, only a fourth of the mothers with no unmet needs scored low, as did a fifth of the mothers with one or two needs and over half of the mothers who said they lacked three or more community services. (p less than .001)

5. Mother's Health

The fifth variable contributing to the variance in the scores was the mother's health. As can be seen in Table 8-10, the better her physical health, as described by the young mother, the greater the likelihood of a high score on overall success. Over half of the mothers who reported their health as excellent scored high, as compared with about a third of those who said their health was good and only about a fifth of the women who reported their health as "fair" or "poor." Almost two-fifths of the mothers in this "fair/poor" category scored very low, as against about a seventh who said their health was good and a tenth of those who reported excellent health.

Table 8-10
Success and Mother's Health

| Success | Mother's Health | | |
	Excellent (N=91)	Good (N=231)	Fair, Poor (N=65)
Very high	25%	15%	11%
High	29	20	11
Moderate	25	28	18
Low	12	23	23
Very low	9	14	37

$x^2 = 38.66$, 8 d.f., p less than .001

6. Resources Used

As had been found in the regression analysis of the mothers' contentment scores when the children were 3 years old, the number of community resources that the mother used was also significant, acccounting for 3% of the variance in overall success scores. The differences were most evident at the extremes. As resource utilization increased, so did the proportions scoring very high; as utilization decreased, the proportions scoring very low increased. (p less than .05)

7. Attitude Toward Pregnancy

The seventh significant variable was the mother's attitude toward her pregnancy, as reported at the Time 1 interview. Almost half the mothers whose attitudes had been positive scored high, as compared with a third of the mothers whose attitudes were ambivalent and a fourth of those mothers who had negative attitudes. As had been found at Time 3 on contentment scores, among the low scoring mothers the major difference was between the mothers with positive attitudes and those whose attitudes were ambivalent or negative. (p less than .01)

D. Ease of Child Care at Time 3

Associations between the mother's difficulty in child care and variables contributing to score variance were examined at two points--when her child was 1½ years old and again at 3. The care of a 1½-year-old child is easier for some women than that of a more active, more independent older child. It was anticipated that the variables contributing to the ease or difficulty of child care at the two points in time would be different, and this was indeed the case.

Mothers who said they found childrearing difficult frequently were impatient and wished they did not have the burden of caring for a child. They had found the mothering role easier when the child was younger and enjoyed the child less at 3. At the other extreme were mothers who took the maternal role in stride. Child care rarely was troublesome for them; they enjoyed the child at the age of 3 as much as or more than they had when she or he was younger.

Four variables accounted for 14% of the variance in the mother's scores on difficulty in caring for a 3-year-old. These were the mother's psychiatric impairment; her reliance on corporal punishment; permissiveness with her child; and resource needs.

1. Psychiatric Impairment

The variable of mother's psychiatric impairment accounted for 15% of the variance in the scores on child care ease. The impairment also had been the strongest indicator of the mother's contentment as well as her overall success score.

Although differences between mothers with low or moderate impairment were minimal, considerable differ- ence was found between highly impaired mothers and those in the other two groups. Far fewer highly impaired mothers found child care easy at Time 3 and far more of these mothers found childrearing hard. Over half of the highly impaired mothers had difficulty caring for a 3-year- old, as compared with about a fourth of the moderately impaired mothers and less than a fifth of the mothers with no or minimal psychiatric impairment. (p less than .001)

2. Corporal Punishment

The degree of corporal punishment the mother used accounted for 4% of the variance in scores on child care ease. The relationship was similar to the association earlier reported between corporal punishment and success scores. The greater the use of corporal punishment, the more difficulty in child care.

Over two-fifths of the mothers who used corporal punishment to a high or excessive degree found child care at age 3 hard. This was in contrast to a third of the mothers who were moderate users and only a fifth of those mothers who used corporal punishment the least. Over a third of the low users of corporal punishment found child care comparatively easy, in contrast to a fifth of the mothers who relied heavily on corporal punishment. (p less than .01)

3. Permissiveness

The third variable responsible for variance in the mothers' scores on the ease of child care was permissiveness. As had been found for mothers scoring high in contentment at Time 3, the relationship among mothers who found child care easy and permissiveness was linear. Two-fifths of the mothers who placed comparatively high restrictions on the child found child care at Time 3 easy in contrast to about a fourth of the mothers who were moderately strict and less than a fifth of the mothers who were highly permissive. Among mothers who found their child care role hard, no difference was found between the low and moderately permissive mothers. However, over half the highly permissive mothers found child care hard, in contrast to a fourth of the highly restrictive mothers. (p less than .001)

4. Resource Needs

The fourth and final variable affecting the mothers' scores on child care ease at Time 3 concerned the availability of helpful community resources, a variable also contributing to the variance in the mother's contentment and overall success score. Over a third of the mothers who expressed no need for additional services found child care easy, but this was true for less than a fourth of the mothers who expressed need for three or more community services not available. Among mothers who found child care difficult, there was little difference between the proportions reporting one or more needs. However, a third or more of the mothers who said they needed one or more services found child care hard, but this was true for less than a fifth of the mothers who reported no community services needed that were not available. (p less than .01)

E. Ease of Child Care at Time 2

This outcome measure assessed the relative difficulty or ease of the mother as parent when her child was 1½. It was composed of most of the items contained in the Time 3 measure.

Only one of the four variables that contributed to the variance in ease in taking care of her 3-year-old was also significant at Time 2. This was the mother's perceived need for community supports or services. Four other variables that were significant at the time the child was 1½ years old were the mother's coping capacity, support from others during her child's infancy, her attitude toward her pregnancy, and her age at the time of her baby's birth. These five variables contributed 21% of the variance to this Time 2 measure of child care ease.

1. Mother's Coping Capacity

The strongest relationship, accounting for 12% of the variance, was the mother's ego strength or ability to cope, a variable also contributing significantly to the variance in

136

the mother's contentment scores at Time 2. The relationship between coping capacity and ease in caring for the 1½-year-old child was linear. Among those mothers who found child care easy, only 12% scored low in coping capacity, as compared with about a fourth of the mothers with middle range scores and two-fifths of the mothers who scored high.

Very few (2%) of those mothers who found child care hard at Time 2 scored high in coping capacity. On the other hand, over a tenth of the middle range mothers and a fourth of the mothers with low coping capacities found child care hard. (p less than .001)

2. Resource Needs

A variable contributing 5% of the variance in the mothers' scores was the perceived need of unavailable community resources. As in the findings pertaining to the ease of care when the child was 3, far fewer mothers who had no unmet needs found child care hard when the child was 18 months old. These mothers were far more likely to have found child care easy than were mothers who desired one or more unavailable community services. (p less than .01)

3. Familial Supports During Child's Infancy

It was hypothesized that the degree of familial and extra-familial supports would influence the parenting. Indices were developed for supports prior to the child's birth as well as during the three interview periods. Cross-tabulations of each form of support with other variables revealed no clear-cut relationships. Only the index reflecting informal supports for the mother shortly after the baby's birth was used in the regression analysis. This index contained 12 items relating to assistance by mother's family and the baby's father, and help in specific aspects of child care.

Informal support during the child's infancy contributed 2% to the mothers' scores in the ease of the child care role when the child was 18 months old.

137

Table 8-11
Ease of Child Care at Time 2 and Early Familial Supports

	Degree of Support		
Child Care	Low (N=69)	Moderate (N=224)	High (N=101)
Easy	26%	26%	18%
Moderate	65	64	58
Hard	9	10	24

$$x^2 = 13.44, \text{ 4 d.f., } p \text{ less than } .01$$

As shown in Table 8-11, there were no differences among those mothers who received minimal or moderate support. About a tenth of these mothers found child care hard. However, among mothers who received the most help in caring for their infants, about a fourth of them had difficulty in taking care of the child at Time 2.

4. Mother's Attitude Toward Pregnancy

The fourth significant variable in the mother's view of ease of child care at Time 2 was her initial attitude toward her pregnancy. This variable also was significant in the mother's contentment at Time 3 and the overall success score. Although the relationship between the mother's attitude and childcaring ease was linear, it was among mothers at the two extremes that differences were most apparent. Whereas a third of the mothers who had very positive attitudes toward the pregnancy found child care easy at Time 2, this was true for less than a fifth of the mothers whose attitudes had been very negative. Conversely, less than a tenth of the mothers with very positive attitudes found child care hard, and over a fourth of the mothers who had very negative attitudes found child care to be difficult. (p less than .05)

5. Mother's Age at Baby's Birth

The final variable that was found significant on the regression analysis and that added to the variance in difficulty in caring for the child at Time 2 was the mother's age at the baby's birth. As can be seen in Table 8-12, the relationship was not linear. Proportionately more of the mothers under 17 when the baby was born were having problems in caring for their child. A third of the 17- and 18-year-old mothers found child care easy, in contrast to less than a fourth of the mothers who were either younger or older at the time of the baby's birth.

Table 8-12
Ease of Child Care at Time 2 and
Mother's Age at Baby's Birth

| Child Care | Mother's Age | | |
	Under 17 (N=33)	17,18 (N=80)	19 & Over (N=284)
Easy	24%	34%	22%
Moderate	52	57	65
Hard	24	9	13

x^2 = 9.36, 4 d.f., p N.S.

F. Disillusionment With Motherhood

Since many of the women entered motherhood at a young age, presumably unprepared to settle down to a more routine and less carefree existence, a disillusionment index was developed from the mother's responses to four items relating to her feelings about her role as parent when her child was 3 years old.

Mothers scoring high on the disillusionment index felt inadequate or overburdened, or disliked the maternal role. They frequently felt guilty about inadequate provision for their child's intellectual growth. These mothers also had found childrearing less rewarding than anticipated. Three variables accounted for 20% of the variance on this measure. These were the mother's psychiatric impairment, the child's sex and the child's health.

139

1. Psychiatric Impairment

The mother's psychiatric impairment accounted for 18% of the variance. There was a linear relationship and the higher the impairment, the greater the disillusionment. About a tenth of the mothers who scored low on impairment were highly disillusioned with their parenting role, in contrast to about a fifth of the mothers of moderate impairment and over two-fifths of the highly impaired mothers. Over a third of the low impairment mothers scored low in disillusionment, as compared with less than a fifth of the highly impaired mothers. (p less than .001)

2. Child's Sex

Sex of the child accounted for 1% of the variance in disillusionment scores. There was no difference among the highly disillusioned mothers, but proportionately more of the mothers with girls than those with boys scored low in disillusionment (Table 8-13).

Table 8-13
Disillusionment and Sex of Child

| | Sex | |
| | Girl | Boy |
Disillusionment	(N=185)	(N=225)
Low	31%	20%
Moderate	36	44
High	33	36
$x^2 = 6.09$, 2 d.f., p less than .05		

3. Child's Health

The final variable contributing to variance on disillusionment was the child's health as reported by the mother when the child was 18 months old. Two-thirds of the children were described as in good health and as having had no illnesses in the preceding 6 months. Twenty-three

140

percent of the children had minor problems such as occasional colds, viruses and other upper respiratory conditions. The children classified as having several or severe health problems were not necessarily in seriously poor health, but were less healthy than the others. They suffered from, for example, frequent or recurrent upper respiratory problems. A few had severe allergies that involved special diets and medication, and some had heart anomalies that required surgery.

As shown in Table 8-14, no differences in degree of disillusionment were found among mothers who had children with no or minor problems. However, mothers of over two-fifths of the children in the poorest health category scored high in disillusionment, in contrast to a fourth of the mothers of children in the two other health categories.

Table 8-14
Disillusionment and Child's Health

	Child's Health		
Disillusionment	No Problem (N=276)	Minor Problem (N=94)	Several or Severe Problems (N=38)
Low	25%	29%	18%
Moderate	52	44	37
High	23	27	45

x^2 = 9.90, 4 d.f., p less than .05

II. VARIABLES ASSOCIATED WITH THE CHILDREN'S ADJUSTMENT

The well-being of a mother and the well-being of her very young child are so intertwined that it seems likely that their adjustments will correspond closely. Since the two are separate persons, and since data on the children's adjustment were available, it seemed desirable to test this assumption.

141

During the 3-year study, the mothers were the primary informants. The interviewers were social workers and could provide general impressions about the children, but were not trained in observational techniques. Since budgetary limitations precluded use of other personnel skilled in these techniques, the study relied on data obtained from the mothers by the interviewers.

The Louisville Behavior Check List, an instrument suitable for use with 3-year-olds, was used in the third year of data collection. It contains 164 true-false questions, covering deviant behavior in children between the ages of 3 and 13. Form E1, designed for children between 3 and 6, was adapted for this sample. The test measures 19 aspects of deviance.

A weakness of the test is that the response to each question is used to indicate deviancy or nondeviancy in several of the measures. Examination of the test results revealed that many of these measures were both redundant and inconclusive as evaluators of the study population. For the study's purposes, the measures retained dealt with aggression, inhibition, cognitive disability, normal irritability, prosocial deficit, neurotic behavior, somatic behavior, and the severity level scale.

As noted, the data were provided by the mother, and bias may influence factual responses.

The eight outcome measures and the significant variables in each are presented in order of degree of variance accounted for.

A. Severity Level

This broad scale of 92 questions included all the noxious and pathogenic behaviors on the checklist. It contained those items included under the separate scales measuring aggression, neurotic behavior, inhibition, somatic behavior and prosocial deficit. Because of its inclusiveness, it was the most potent direct measure of the child's adjustment. The severity level was a summarized measure of a child's disturbed behavior.

142

Four variables accounted for 25% of the variance in the severity scores: the mother's contentment, the child's health, the mother's reliance on corporal punishment, and the mother's impairment.

1. The Mother's Contentment

The mother's contentment at Time 3 was entered as an independent variable in the children's adjustment measures. The index, described earlier, measures the mother's sense of well-being and contentment as parent.

It had the strongest relationship with the severity level of the children, accounting for 14% of the variance. As shown in Table 8-15, the more contented the mother was, the more likely her child would have few, if any, symptoms of maladjustment. A third of the highly contented mothers had children who were relatively symptom-free, in contrast to 16% of the children of the moderately contented mothers and a tenth of the children of mothers of low contentment.

Table 8-15
Severity Level Scores and Mother's Contentment

Severity Level Scores (Degree of Malajustment)	Degree of Contentment		
	High (N=133)	Moderate (N=157)	Low (N=119)
None, minimal	32%	16%	10%
Moderate	58	66	58
Severe	10	18	32

$$x^2 = 34.95, 2 \text{ d.f., p less than } .001$$

2. The Child's Health

Accounting for 7% of the variance in the children's test scores was the child's health at 1½ years, as reported by the mother. No difference was seen among children

143

with no health problems and those with minimal problems. Discernible differences emerged, however, when children with several or severe health problems were compared with children in the other two groups. Having several or severe health problems was clearly associated with maladjustment. Only 5% of these children, as compared with a fifth of the other children, had scores indicating they were relatively problem-free. Over two-fifths of the children with several or severe health problems were in the severely maladjusted group (Table 8-16).

Table 8-16
Severity Level Scores and Child's Health

	Child's Health		
			Several or
	No	Minor	Severe
Severity Level Scores	Problem	Problem	Problems
(Degree of Malajustment)	(N=275)	(N=94)	(N=39)
None, minimal	21%	19%	5%
Moderate	64	59	51
Severe	15	22	44

$$x^2 = 24.77, \text{ 4 d.f., p less than } .001$$

3. Corporal Punishment

The third significant variable was the mother's use of corporal punishment. As can be seen in Table 8-17, the less corporal punishment, the more likely that the child had no or minimal problems of maladjustment. A third of the children of mothers who resorted to corporal punishment seldom if ever, were problem-free, as compared with a fifth of the children of mothers who placed moderate reliance on corporal punishment and a tenth of the children of heavy users. Among the severely maladjusted children, there was no difference between the children of mothers using low or moderate corporal punishment. However, children of mothers who relied heavily on corporal punishment were overrepresented in this category.

144

Table 8-17
Severity Level Scores and
Mother's Use of Corporal Punishment

Severity Level Scores (Degree of Maladjustment)	Use of Corporal Punishment		
	Low (N=127)	Moderate (N=164)	High (N=117)
None, minimal	32%	18%	9%
Moderate	54	65	63
Severe	14	17	28

x^2 = 25.39, 4 d.f., p less than .001

4. The Mother's Impairment

The fourth influential variable was the mother's psychiatric impairment, a variable of paramount significance in five of the six mother's outcome measures. The association between high impairment of the mother and severe maladjustment of the child is apparent in Table 8-18. A third of the children of mothers who were highly impaired had severe adjustment problems, as compared with slightly over a tenth of the children of mothers in the other two groups. Only 6% of the children of mothers with high impairment were found in the category of no or minimal maladjustment, in contrast to well over a fifth of the children of the other mothers.

Table 8-18
Severity Level Scores and Mother's Impairment

Severity Level Scores (Degree of Maladjustment)	Mother's Impairment		
	Low (N=143)	Moderate (N=123)	High (N=143)
None, minimal	30%	23%	6%
Moderate	57	64	62
Severe	13	13	32

x^2 = 38.96, 4 d.f., p less than .001

B. Normal Irritability

This scale described noxious behaviors such as being overdemanding, hyperactive, bossy and complaining, reported to occur in at least 25% of the general population. Children scoring high on this test were likely to have difficulty in peer relationships, to want more than their due, and possibly to have difficulty in relationships with adults.

Four variables were significant, explaining 23% of the variance on the normal irritability scores. They were mother's contentment, use of corporal punishment, child's sex, and mother's symptoms during pregnancy.

1. The Mother's Contentment

The mother's contentment with herself and with her parenting role contributed 17% of the variance in the children's normal irritability scores. There was a direct relationship and the higher the mother's contentment, the more the child's freedom from noxious behaviors. A third of the children of highly contented mothers exhibited few if any such behavior symptoms, in contrast to a fifth of the children of moderately contented mothers and less than a tenth of the children of the most discontented women. Over two-fifths of the mothers who scored low in contentment had children with many distasteful behavior characteristics, in contrast to less than a fifth of the rest of the sample. (p less than .001)

2. Corporal Punishment

The second variable--corporal punishment--contributed 3% to the variance in the children's scores. The children of mothers who rarely used corporal punishment were clearly more symptom-free. Almost a third of these children scored low on normal irritability, as compared with less than a fifth of the other children. (p less than .01)

146

3. The Child's Sex

The child's sex contributed 2% to the variance on the normal irritability scores. As can be seen in Table 8-19, over a third of the boys, as compared with about a fourth of the girls, were reported to be relatively symptom-free on this test.

Table 8-19
Child's Normal Irritability Score and Child's Sex

	Sex of Child	
	Girl	Boy
Normal Irritability Scores	(N=184)	(N=226)
Low	24%	35%
Moderate	39	36
High	37	29

x^2 = 6.09, 2 d.f., p less than .05

4. The Mother's Symptoms

The fourth variable reflected the mother's report on symptoms during her pregnancy, the data being obtained from the mothers at the Time 1 interview. The index consisted of six items concerned with physical and emotional symptoms during the pregnancy, such as headaches, nausea, fatigue, irritability, depression and special food cravings.

The relationship between the number of symptoms reported and the children's test scores on normal irritability was linear. The fewer the symptoms reported, the more likely that the child scored low. As shown in Table 8-20, over a fourth of the children of mothers who reported few symptoms were themselves relatively symptom-free, in contrast to 22% of the children of mothers reporting moderate symptoms and 12% of the children of high symptom mothers.

147

Table 8-20
Child's Normal Irritability Score and Mother's Symptoms

| | Number of Symptoms | | |
| | Few | Moderate | Many |
Normal Irritability Scores	(N=122)	(N=171)	(N=117)
Low	27%	22%	12%
Moderate	57	56	53
High	16	22	35

$$x^2 = 16.85, \text{ 4 d.f., p less than } .01$$

C. Aggression

Thirty-eight questions were used to measure aggression displayed by the child. The questions were directed to the child's egocentric, emotionally demanding and interpersonally belligerent behavior. The scale included questions about the child's ability to share, relationship with other children and adults, and antisocial behavior. Low scorers would tend to have achieved a social development that includes the "we" as well as the "I" in their thoughts and behavior. A low rating on this scale in no way indicates a lack of initiative or a tendency to be overly compliant.

Four variables were significant and together accounted for 22% of the variance in the scores. These were the mother's contentment, the mother's reliance on corporal punishment, the child's health and the mother's psychiatric impairment.

1. The Mother's Contentment

The strongest relationship, accounting for 14% of the variance in the aggression scores, was the mother's contentment. The relationship was linear. Almost half of the children of mothers who had very positive feelings about themselves and their role as parent scored low, as compared with about a third of the children of moderately contented mothers and less than a fifth of the children

148

whose mothers were least contented. Conversely, the higher the mother's contentment, the less likely was her child to score high in aggression. (p less than .001)

2. Corporal Punishment

Corporal punishment accounted for 4% of the variance in aggression scores. Over half of the children of mothers who rarely if ever used corporal punishment scored low on aggression. This was the case for about a fourth of the children of mothers comparatively moderate in using this form of discipline and for a fifth of the children of mothers who used corporal punishment to a high degree. A fourth of the children whose mothers used corporal punishment rarely if at all were in this category, as compared with a third of the children of moderate users and two-fifths of the children of mothers who used corporal punishment more extensively. (p less than .001)

3. The Child's Health

The third variable, adding 2% to the variance in aggression scores, was the child's health. The fewer the health problems, the lower the aggression score, and the converse. About two-fifths of the children who had no health problems scored low on aggression, in contrast to less than a fourth of the children whose health was most precarious. Among the most sickly children almost two-thirds scored high on aggression, as compared with about a fourth of the healthiest children. (p less than .001)

4. The Mother's Psychiatric Impairment

Another variable that contributed significantly to the variance in the aggression scores was the mother's psychiatric impairment. A direct relationship was found. Whereas half of the children of highly impaired mothers scored high in aggression, less than a third of the children of moderately impaired mothers and only a fifth of the children of mothers with low impairment were in this category. Among children who scored low in aggression, the difference between children whose mothers had little or moderate impairment was not significant. However, whereas about two-fifths or more of these children scored low in aggression, this was true for less than a fifth of the children of mothers who were highly impaired. (p less than .001)

D. Neurotic Behavior

The 20 questions included in this measure described such symptoms as phobias, obsessions and fears. Children ranked high in neurotic behavior are described as fearful of riding in automobiles, of storms, the dark, dirt and germs, and of sleeping alone. They may have separation problems when their parents go out, and they are likely to over-react to pain. High scorers may also have tics, engage in ritualistic behavior, and become excessively upset by a change in routine.

The study children were divided into three categories--no symptoms, moderate symptoms and high symptoms. Of the 410 children on whom data were available, a fourth (24%) were reported to have no symptoms. Fifty-seven percent were reported as having from one to three neurotic symptoms and were classified as moderately impaired. Nineteen percent had four or more symptoms and were classified as high in symptomatology.

Five variables accounted for 21% of the variance in scores. They were mother's contentment, child's health, mother's symptoms during pregnancy, her use of corporal punishment, and the sex of the child.

1. The Mother's Contentment

The mother's contentment accounted for 11% of the variance in the children's scores. The relationship between the mother's contentment and the child's neurotic symptoms was linear. Whereas almost two-fifths of the children of mothers who were most contented were reported to have no neurotic symptoms, this was the case for only a fifth of the children of moderately contented women and for only about a tenth of the children of the least contented mothers. Among those children with the most neurotic symptoms the distribution was in the reverse. A third of the children of the least contented women were in this category, as compared with less than a fifth of the children of moderately contented mothers and with only a tenth of the children of the mothers who were most contented. (p less than .001)

2. The Child's Health

The child's physical health contributed 4% to the variance on this outcome measure. The relationship between health and neurotic symptoms score was most apparent at the two extremes--children with no health problems and children with several or severe problems. Whereas 28% of the children with no health problems were reported free of neurotic symptoms, this was true for only 2% of the children who had several or severe health problems. Less than a fifth of the children with no health problems scored high on neurotic symptoms, in contrast to almost a third of the children with the most severe health problems. (p less than .01)

3. The Mother's Symptoms

The variable on symptoms the mother reported during pregnancy accounted for 3% of the variance in neurotic behavior scores. The fewer the symptoms the mother reported, the more likely that her child had no neurotic symptoms. Conversely, the more pregnancy symptoms reported, the more likely that the child scored high. About two-fifths of the children of mothers who reported few pregnancy symptoms were reported to have no neurotic symptoms. This compares with about a fourth of the children of mothers with a moderate number of pregnancy symptoms and a tenth of the children of the high symptom mothers. (p less than .001)

151

4. Corporal Punishment

The extent that the mother used corporal punishment was a variable also significant in relation to neurotic behavior. Among children with no neurotic symptoms, no difference was found between children of mothers who used corporal punishment rarely and those who used it moderately. However, proportionately fewer of the children whose mothers used corporal punishment frequently were reported to have no neurotic symptoms. Among children in the high symptom category, only a tenth of the children of mothers who rarely used corporal punishment scored high on neurotic symptoms, as contrasted with a fifth of the children of moderate users and over a fourth of the children of mothers who relied heavily on corporal punishment. (p less than .01)

5. The Child's Sex

The final variable, the child's sex, added 2% to the variance in the scores. As in the normal irritability scores, the boys scored better than the girls. Whereas 29% of the boys were reported to be free of neurotic symptoms, this was true for only 17% of the girls. (p less than .02)

E. Inhibition

The degree of the child's inhibition was measured by the mother's response to 35 questions concerned with the child's interest in interacting with others, her or his feelings of being liked, ability to respond to stress with nonrivalrous behavior, and freedom from manifest anxiety about self. Children scoring high on inhibition were likely to be frightened, dependent, and unable to stand up for their rights.

In the regression analysis, four variables were found significant, and together accounted for 19% of the variance in the inhibition scores. These variables are mother's contentment, child's health, child's sex, and parental permissiveness.

152

1. The Mother's Contentment

Mother's contentment accounted for 13% of the variance in inhibition scores. The higher the mother's contentment, the more likely that her child had few symptoms of inhibition. The converse was also true. Over two-fifths of the very contented mothers had children who scored low on inhibition, in contrast to less than a third of the children of moderately contented mothers and only a seventh of the children of mothers ranked low in contentment. Among children who scored high on inhibition, the distributions were in the opposite direction, with far more children of low contentment mothers found in this category of disturbance. (p less than .001)

2. The Child's Health

The child's health added 3% to the variance in the inhibition scores. Whereas a third of the most healthy children scored low on inhibition, this was true for a fourth of the moderately healthy children, but for less than a tenth of the children with the most health problems. Among the children high in inhibition, a fifth were children with no health problems, in contrast to over two-fifths of the least healthy children. (p less than .01)

3. The Child's Sex

Sex also proved a variable of significance in inhibition. As with the normal irritability and neurotic behavior scores, the boys scored better on inhibition than did the girls. Over a third of the boys scored low on this test, in contrast to only about a fifth of the girls. Girls tended to be slightly more highly represented in the moderate category. The differences among the boys and girls scoring high on inhibition were minimal. (p less than .01)

4. Parental Permissiveness

The fourth variable adding to the variance on the inhibition scores is the degree of the mother's permissiveness. This variable included such items as the mother's expectations regarding the child's treatment of furniture and other objects in the home, and her expectations regarding compliance with parental demands and limitations. Parental permissiveness was a significant variable in three of the mother's outcome measures. In each instance it was found that the less permissive the mother, the better the outcome.

As can be seen in Table 8-21, a different pattern was found in relation to the children's inhibition scores. Half of the mothers who placed moderate restrictions on their children had children who scored low on inhibition, in contrast to less than two-fifths of the children of mothers who placed minimal and high restrictions on their child's behavior. In other words, moderately permissive parents tended to produce children who had low inhibition scores.

Table 8-21
Inhibition Scores and Parental Permissiveness

| Inhibition Score | Parental Permissiveness | | |
	High (N=114)	Moderate (N=154)	Low (N=140)
Low	39%	51%	35%
Moderate, high	61	49	65

$$x^2 = 8.53, \ 2 \ \text{d.f.}, \ p \ \text{less than} \ .02$$

F. Cognitive Disability

This measure contained 24 questions dealing with the child's ability to master age-specific cognitive tasks. Questions related to the child's emotional and physical developmental levels were also included. The child's ability to count to five, sing TV commercials or recite a nursery rhyme, correctly identify at least one color, climb, or throw a ball, were some of the items covered.

Four variables were found to be significantly related to this measure of the child's physical, mental and

154

emotional development. These variables--the child's health, the mother's contentment, the mother's use of corporal punishment, and the mother's symptoms during her pregnancy--accounted for 11% of the variance in the scores.

1. The Child's Health

The child's health explained 5% of the variance in scores. Among children in the high scoring group, the major difference was between those in the poorest health category and children with no or only minor health problems. A fourth of the children reported to have severe and/or numerous health problems were in the most severely disabled category in regard to physical, mental and emotional development. This was true for less than a tenth of the children in the other two health categories. (p less than .01)

2. The Mother's Contentment

An additional 3% of the variance in the children's cognitive disability scores was due to the variable, mother's contentment. Little difference was found among children who scored low and moderate on cognitive disability. The major difference was among the children who scored high. Whereas only a tenth of the children of highly contented mothers scored high on this measure, this was the case for a fourth of the children of least contented mothers. (p less than .05)

3. Corporal Punishment

The mother's reliance on corporal punishment was also found to be significant and explained 2% of the variance in the children's scores on cognitive disability. Little difference was found between children of mothers who used corporal punishment to a low degree and those who used it moderately. However, a fourth of the children of mothers who rarely used corporal punishment scored low

155

in cognitive disability, in contrast to a tenth of the children of mothers who were high users. Among the children who scored high in cognitive disability, the proportions were reversed. (p less than .01)

4. Mother's Symptoms

The final variable found significant was the mother's recall of the physical and emotional symptoms experienced during pregnancy. Although there were no differences among the low and moderate scoring children, among children with many symptoms of cognitive disability a considerable difference was seen between children of mothers who had many symptoms during pregnancy and those who had moderate or few symptoms. Well over a fourth of the children of mothers who reported many pregnancy symptoms versus slightly over a tenth of the children of mothers in the low or moderate groups had high cognitive disability scores. (p less than .01)

G. Somatic Behavior

Twelve questions, the total number used in the original clinical scale, were included in this measure. The scale, which has items reflecting both structural and functional disability, measures somatic dysfunction related to brain damage or psychic stress. Two-fifths of the children in the study were reported to be free of any symptoms included under somatic behavior. They were in good health, had no severe physical handicaps and no problems with bladder or bowel control. They were not troubled with asthma, frequent headaches, stomachaches or with other somatic disorders that may be related to brain damage or to psychic stress. An additional two-fifths had one or two symptoms and the rest were reported to have three or more.

Four variables were found to be significant in the regression analysis. They were the child's health, the mother's psychiatric impairment, the child's sex, and the degree of corporal punishment used by the mother. The variables, combined, accounted for 11% of the variance in the children's test scores.

156

1. Child's Health

The variable of child's health explained 5% of the variance in the somatic behavior scores. Since the scale reflected health status, this was not surprising. No difference was found between children with no health problems and those with only minor problems. However, whereas over two-fifths of the healthier children were reported to have no symptoms of somatic behavior, this was true for only a fifth of the children in the poorest health category. (p less than .05)

2. The Mother's Psychiatric Impairment

The mother's psychiatric impairment accounted for 3% of the variance. Mothers with low or moderate impairment were equally likely to have children with no symptoms of somatic behavior disorders. About half of their children were symptom-free, in contrast to a fourth of the children of mothers with a high degree of psychiatric impairment. Conversely, a far higher proportion of children of mothers with high impairment, as compared with children of mothers with moderate or low impairment, had three or more symptoms of somatic behavior. (p less than .001)

3. The Child's Sex

The third variable, sex of the child, accounted for 2% of the variance in the somatic behavior scores. Unlike the previous categories where sex was significant, on this test it was the girls rather than the boys who proved more problem-free. More than two-fifths of the girls had no symptoms or somatic behavior disorder; this was the case for only about a third of the boys. (p less than .05)

4. Corporal Punishment

The fourth and final variable was the amount of corporal punishment used by the mother. Almost half of the children whose mothers rarely if ever used corporal punishment had no somatic symptoms, in contrast to only two-fifths of the children of the moderate users and a third of the children of mothers who used corporal punishment extensively or exclusively. (p less than .05)

H. Prosocial Deficit

The prosocial deficit scale measured the extent to which the child's behavior was in accord with what is expected in society. Children who were considerate and desirous of doing well, relaxed, not easily upset, in good health and enjoyed contact with children their age were rated as having no deficits. Over two-fifths (44%) of the children in this study were reported to possess these and other positive characteristics, and an additional 29% were reported deficient in only one of the characteristics measured by the test.

Perhaps because of the one-sided distribution, only three variables were found significant in the multiple regression analysis, accounting for only 10% of the variance in the children's test scores. The three variables were the mother's contentment, the child's health, and the degree of corporal punishment.

1. The Mother's Contentment

Six percent of the variance was accounted for by the mother's contentment. The degree of contentment was clearly associated with the number of prosocial deficits observed by the mother in her child. The higher the mother's contentment, the more likely that she reported her child to have no deficits. Similarly, the lower her contentment the more likely that her child was reported to have two or more deficits. Over half of the children of highly contented mothers had no deficits, as compared with less than half of the children of moderately contented women and only a third of those of women in the low contentment category. The children of two-fifths of the poorly contented mothers had two or more prosocial deficits, as compared with a fourth of the children of the

158

moderately contented mothers and with 15% of the children of the highly contented mothers. (p less than .001)

2. The Child's Health

The child's health explained an additional 3% of the variance in this adjustment measure. That poor health was included as one of the eight indicators of maladjustment in this prosocial deficit scale may in part explain the presence of this independent variable in the multiple regression. However, it appears unlikely that this one indicator would totally explain the variance between the independent and dependent variables.

It was evident that the better the child's health, the more likely the child had no prosocial deficits. Half of the children with no health problems had no prosocial deficits, as compared with two-fifths of the children with minor health problems and a fourth of the children in the most serious health categories. The proportion of children in the poorest health category who had two or more deficits was twice that of the children with no health problems. (p less than .05)

3. Corporal Punishment

The third variable accounting for the variance on the prosocial deficit scores was the degree to which the mother used corporal punishment. The less this type of discipline was utilized, the more likely that the child was reported to have no deficits. Whereas over half the children of mothers who used corporal punishment rarely if ever had no deficits, only about two-fifths of the children of moderate users and about one-third of the children of high users were so reported. Among those with two or more deficits, the reverse linear association was found. The less the use of corporal punishment, the smaller the proportion of children with two or more deficits. (p less than .05)

SUMMARY AND DISCUSSION OF THE FINDINGS

This chapter has examined outcome measures reflecting the well-being of the mothers and their children, and the variables associated with these measures. This section presents a summary and discussion of the findings on the mothers' outcomes, and then a summary and discussion of variables associated with the children's adjustment.

The Mothers

Two outcomes concerned the specific ease or difficulty the mother experienced in her caretaking role when her child was 1½, and then 3 years old. Three measures--one at Time 2 and two at Time 3--were more global indicators of the mother's feelings about herself and her role as parent. The sixth outcome measure, developed to assess the degree of successful coping over time, included four of the already mentioned measures, and observations made by the interviewers with regard to the parenting provided by the mothers.

A total of 13 independent variables were found to be significant in explaining variances of the six outcome measures. The degree of the mother's psychiatric impairment and the number of perceived but unavailable resource needs were each found significant on five outcome measures. The mother's attitude toward her pregnancy and her degree of permissiveness in matters of child care were significantly related to three outcome variables. The mother's coping capacity, the degree to which she relied on corporal punishment in child behavior management, and the number of community resources she had used to enhance her maternal role added to the explained variance on two outcome variables. Other independent variables, significant on only one of the six outcome measures, were the mother's age at the time of her baby's birth, the degree of early familial support, the mother's physical health, the child's sex and health status, the mother's pleasure in mothering an infant, and the absence or presence of a husband or male partner in the home.

The most powerful variable, contributing from 12% to 40% of the variance in all but one of the six outcome scores, was the degree of the mother's impairment as measured by the Langner six-item index of psychiatric

160

impairment. Mothers who scored low on impairment were more contented, felt more adequate in and reconciled to their maternal role, found the task of childrearing when their child was 3 years of age relatively easy, and scored higher on the overall measure of successful outcome than did mothers who exhibited a high degree of psychiatric impairment. The relationship between the mothers' psychiatric impairment and the outcome scores is not surprising. It is reassuring insofar as it supports the validity of the outcome measures. On the other hand, since no measure of psychiatric impairment prior to motherhood was available, questions of causality and circularity arise. The absence or presence of psychiatric symptoms on the part of the mothers indeed may predict how well they functioned in the childrearing role and how contented they were to be parents. Yet it is also likely that contented mothers and mothers who find childrearing easy will tend to be less depressed, feel less isolated, be less restless, etc.

The importance of the availability of a variety of community supportive services is evident. The perceived need for such help was found to contribute to the variance in the scores of five of the outcome variables. The more community supports that the mother reported as unavailable but needed, the more likely she found the tasks associated with child care management difficult, the less contented she was, and the more likely she scored low on the overall success score.

Data for the items in the permissiveness index were obtained at Time 3. This independent variable, therefore, was used only in the regression analyses of the three Time 3 outcome variables, as well as in the overall success scores. The degree of the mother's permissiveness added 3% to 8% to the explained variance on three of these outcome measures. The less permissive the mother, the more likely she was to be highly contented, find child care easy, and score high on the overall success score. Although one would anticipate that a position midway between permissiveness and strictness is the sought-for ideal, this was not found to be the case in relation to outcome for the mothers. By being comparatively strict and by maintaining

161

limits on what the child can or cannot do, the mother may be more contented and deal more effectively with her child care role. On the other hand, it is possible that there is the problem of circularity; it may be that the more contented mothers and those who find child care easy are more secure and therefore able to exert a greater amount of control over their children's behavior.

The mother's attitude toward her pregnancy was found to account for a small but significant degree of the variance on three of the outcome measures--the ease with which she viewed her child care tasks when her child was 1½ years of age, her contentment at Time 3, and her overall success score. A more positive attitude toward the pregnancy, as reported by the mother at the interview shortly after her hospital confinement, was associated with a better outcome on these three measures. The fact that the mother's attitudes did not contribute significantly to the variance in the mother's facility for child care task management at Time 3, suggests a diminution in the importance of this variable as the child gets older. However, since the mother's attitude was significantly associated with her contentment at this time period, it is more probable that the attitudinal variables per se become less powerful in explaining the degree of ease in child care management when maternal behavioral variables are entered in the regression. These behavioral variables dealing with the degree of parental permissiveness and use of corporal punishment may, in many instances, reflect the mother's previous and current feelings about her child. That the mother's attitude toward her pregnancy was found to be significant in the mother's overall success score, would indicate, however, that it is relevant to the well-being of the mothers.

A second measure dealing with behavior management, the mother's use of corporal punishment, also was used only in the regression analyses of the Time 3 outcome variables and the overall success scores. Mothers who used corporal punishment the least were more likely to find child care easier and also score higher on the overall success score than were mothers who used corporal punishment to a

162

greater extent. It is true that some children require more punishment than do others and that this could account for the relationship between the use of corporal punishment and ease of child care. On the other hand, the fact that the use of corporal punishment also figures in the overall summary score, coupled with the fact that parental permissiveness was associated with these same outcome variables, suggests that the relationships between the use of corporal punishment and the two dependent variables are explained by the parenting style rather than by the child's behavior.

The use of community resources at Time 3 contributed to the explained variance in the mothers' contentment and overall success scores. The more community resources used, the more likely the mothers to score high on these two outcome variables. That resource use was not associated with the mothers' ease in performing specific child care tasks is of particular interest. The resource usage explored in this independent variable involves resources commonly geared to the better educated, middle class population. An interest and facility in reading are required, as well as an ability to internalize and subsequently utilize general, somewhat abstract, information relating to child development and child care. Among the mothers in this study, the association between resource utilization and education was clearly evident (p less than .001), whereas no association was found between the mother's ease in the performance of her child care tasks and her educational level. It is possible that while this resource utilization may have benefited the more highly educated women, it may have had little effect in providing practical help with child care management for many of the women in this study.

The one outcome measure in which the mother's psychiatric impairment was found not to be significant on the regression analysis was the ease with which the mother viewed child care at Time 2. In this instance it was the mother's coping capacity, as measured by the Thomas-Zander Ego Strength Scale, that was the most powerful variable, explaining 12% of the variance in the mothers'

163

scores. This same independent variable was found to be significant in the regression of the mother's degree of contentment at Time 2. Since the Ego Strength Scale tends to tap established personality characteristics rather than more current emotional patterns as revealed in the psychiatric impairment index, the problem of circularity is diminished. It is reasonable to conclude that the internal strengths that the mother brings to her parenting role make her more contented and make it easier for her to perform her child care tasks.

Seven other variables were found to be significant in each instance only in relation to one outcome measure. Women who derived a high degree of pleasure from mothering an infant and women who lived with their husband or a male partner at Time 2 were more contented at that time than were women whose pleasure in such mothering was moderate or low and those women who lived alone or with other than a husband or male partner. Neither of these independent variables was significant at Time 3.

Not unexpectedly, mothers of children with several or severe health problems were likely to score high in disillusionment with regard to their role as parent. Less explicable was the finding that mothers with girls were more likely to be less disillusioned with their parenting role than were mothers with boys.

The mother's age at the time of her baby's birth was found to contribute to the explained variance on her ease in child care management at the time her child was 1½ years of age. The youngest mothers, those who were under 17 when their children were born, were more likely to have difficulty coping with child care tasks than those who were 17 years of age or older. However, by the time the children had reached 3, the mother's age was no longer significant. This suggests that the earlier parenting period may be the most difficult for very young mothers, a period when they would be most highly in need of supportive services, including information and counseling directed to child care task management.

The degree of familial support that the mothers received during the very early period of child care also contributed to the variance of the scores on the ease of child care at Time 2. The findings, however, are different from those anticipated. Although no differences were found among mothers who found child care easy or moderately easy, more of the mothers who had received a comparatively high degree of familial support during the early child care period found childrearing difficult when their child was 1½ years old. It well may be that, in many instances, the high degree of help that the mother received in performing child care tasks was counter productive, and that when this help was withdrawn, these women had more difficulty than did others who had been helped moderately or not at all.

The final variable, explaining some of the variance in the mothers' overall success scores, was the mother's health. Not unexpectedly, there was a linear relationship between health and overall success: the better the physical health as reported by the mother, the more likely that her overall outcome score was high.

In summation, 13 variables were found to be significant in contributing to the variance of the six outcome measures of maternal well-being and success. Combinations of from three to seven of these independent variables explained from 20% to 50% of the variance in the outcome measures. The factors most closely related to the mother's adjustment were her psychiatric impairment, her expressed need for unavailable community resources, her permissiveness in child behavior management and her initial attitude toward her pregnancy.

The Children

Seven independent variables were found to be significant in explaining between 10% to 15% of the variance within the eight outcome measures used to assess the children's adjustment when they were 3 years old. The mother's contentment with herself and with her role as parent, the degree that the mother relied on corporal punishment and the child's physical health were each found to be significant on seven outcome measures. The child's sex was significantly associated with four outcome variables. The mother's psychiatric impairment and the number of symptoms that the mother reported having during pregnancy were significant in three of the eight outcome measures. The one other independent variable, significant in one outcome measure, was the mother's permissiveness toward her child.

The most potent variable that appeared influential in contributing toward the child's well-being was the mother's own feelings about herself and about her role as mother. Although the mother's contentment was not significantly related to the child's somatic behavior, it was significant in seven of the eight tests and in all but one instance was the most powerful predictor among the variables. It alone accounted for from 3% to 17% of the variance in the seven other outcome measures.

The more contented the mother, the more likely that her child was problem-free. Likewise, the less contented the mother, the more likely that her child had a comparatively high level of maladjustment as measured by these outcome variables.

The child's health was also significant in seven of the outcome measures and explained the greatest amount of variance in the child's somatic behavior and cognitive disability scores. Usually the differences were most apparent between children in the poorest health category and their peers who had no health problem or whose problems were transient and relatively minor. Children whose health status had been the most precarious at 1½ years of age were likely to have more symptoms of pathology at age 3 than their counterparts. They showed a higher degree of symptomatology on aggression, inhibition, cognitive disability, somatic behavior, prosocial deficit, and severity level scales. Far fewer of them were symptom-free on the neurotic behavior outcome measure, as compared with their peers.

166

The association between the physical health of 1½-year-old children and their well-being 1½ years later was not unexpected. For some children the health problem per se probably created developmental problems. In some instances parental fears and concerns about their child's frequent or serious health problems may have resulted in overprotectiveness or weariness on the part of the mother that in turn created behavioral problems and discouraged normal development. The suggestion that parental attitudes may be associated with caring for the less healthy child was also reflected in the mother's outcome measure on disillusionment. Far more of the mothers who had children with several or severe health problems, as compared with mothers of children in comparatively good health, felt inadequate and overburdened with their parental role.

The third variable that was significant in seven of the eight tests was the degree that the mother relied on corporal punishment in discipline. Mothers who used corporal punishment the least were more likely to have children with few or no symptoms of disturbance. On several of the tests the differences between the scores of children of mothers who used corporal punishment to a moderate or high degree were not significant, but these children generally showed a higher degree of pathology than did children of mothers who rarely if ever used corporal punishment. On the mothers' outcome variables minimal or no corporal punishment was associated with easier child care and higher overall success score. The "spare the rod, spoil the child" adage is certainly contradicted in many of the findings concerned with 3-year-old children and their mothers. In discipline, scoldings, admonitions and other nonphysical punishment may be more productive than spankings and slaps.

The child's sex was associated with the normal irritability, neurotic behavior, inhibition and somatic behavior scores. On all but the last-mentioned, the boys were found to be better adjusted. On the other hand, mothers of girls were more likely to be less disillusioned with

167

parenting than were mothers of boys. Why boys fared better on three outcome measures and girls on one is unclear. Among younger children, the sex of the child reportedly has no effect on the scales.*

The mother's psychiatric impairment was associated with the child's somatic behavior, aggression, and severity level scores. The most highly impaired mother was likely to have a child with high symptomatology on these three tests. Although the association between the mother's impairment and the child's aggression score was linear, the difference between children of mothers of low or moderate psychiatric impairment was not significant in the two other tests.

The number of symptoms the mother had during pregnancy accounted for a small but significant amount of the variances on the child's tests of cognitive disability, normal irritability and neurotic behavior. Mothers who reported many symptoms were most likely to have children who scored high in symptomatology on these three aspects of behavioral and psychological disturbance. As stated earlier, the mother's recollection of symptoms may reflect her mental health and her attitude about pregnancy. These maternal characteristics could affect the child.

Parental permissiveness was significant on the children's inhibition scores. The moderately permissive mothers, as opposed to mothers who were highly permissive or very strict, were more likely to have children who scored well on this test. This finding is somewhat at odds with the earlier findings that a low degree of permissiveness was associated with mothers' outcome. It may be that though strictness is more compatible with the mother's well-being, a milder position is more compatible with the child's well-being.

In summary, seven variables were found to contribute to the variance on the eight measures of child well-being. The three factors most closely related to the child's adjustment were the mother's contentment with herself and with her role as parent, the child's health, and the degree to which the mother used corporal punishment.

* Louisville Behavior Check List Manual, p. 19.

CHAPTER 9
SUMMARY AND DISCUSSION

During the last decade more and more white unwed mothers have chosen to keep their children rather than surrender them for adoption, as in the past. Earlier studies have reported on the disadvantageous position of the unwed mother and her child with regard to health and economic status, as well as personal and social adjustment. Social agencies have expressed concern, fearing that the unwed mother will not be able to sustain her plan, and that the trend to keep the child may result in mother-child separations and requests for agency placement after the child is 2 or 3 years old.

Despite evidence of relaxed standards and changing attitudes toward the woman pregnant out of wedlock, many pregnant women still marry to avoid giving birth out of wedlock. Many "forced" marriages involve teen-age or early postteen-age parents. Children born to young married women are not necessarily guaranteed a stable family structure either.

This study was undertaken by the Child Welfare League of America to explore the deleterious effects of childrearing out of wedlock. It examined the relationship between the mother's marital status at the time of the baby's birth, her age and other maternal characteristics, experiences and attitudes, and the subsequent well-being of mother and child. Do the disadvantages for the unwed mother and child reported at an earlier time still exist? Is the trend to keep the baby only a delayed form of adoption --that is, does the unwed mother need to surrender or at least find subsitute care for her child as the child grows older? Is marital status at the time the baby was born the strongest predictor of outcome for mother and child, or are

169

other variables more closely associated with the mother's and child's well-being?

This chapter presents a brief description of the study design and the principal findings. The implications for policy and practice are then discussed.

STUDY DESIGN

The study was directed to white primiparous women who were under 25 years of age at the time of their first live birth. The study population was obtained through the cooperation of 15 hospitals in Milwaukee County, a maternity home in an adjacent county, and the Wisconsin Department of Health and Social Services. Of the 599 mothers identified as eligible for participation in the study, 448 (75%) were interviewed. Most of those not interviewed either refused to participate or could not be located. In the course of the 3-year period in which the study was in progress, three mothers died and five others permanently surrendered their children for adoption, dropping the study population to 440 mothers and their children.

The mothers were interviewed in their homes within a month after the babies' birth, when the children were 1½ years old, and when the children were 3. The interview schedules contained both open-ended and closed-response questions, exploring various aspects of the mother's past and current experiences and her social and emotional adjustment. Langner's six-item index of psychiatric impairment was used at all three interviews. The Rosenberg Self-Esteem Scale and the Thomas-Zander Ego Strength Scale were administered to the mother at the second and third interviews. The child's adjustment was assessed through the mother's responses to questions from the Louisville Behavior Check List.

Indices were developed to measure the mother's adjustment to her maternal role when her child was 18 months and 3 years old. Eight scales from the Louisville Behavior Check List were used to measure the child's adjustment at age 3. A series of independent variables, including demographic characteristics of the mothers as well as personality and health variables, were then related to each of the outcome measures. Regression analysis was used to assess the relative influence of significant variables on the various measures of outcome.

DESCRIPTION OF THE STUDY POPULATION

The Mothers

The initial study population included 261 married and 187 unmarried women. About a third of the married women had conceived prior to marriage. At the time of the baby's birth, the median age of the mothers was 20.4. The median monthly income was $539; 3 years later it had increased to $815.

Almost three-fourths of the women came from intact homes, and almost always the relationship between the women's parents was regarded as good. Most of the fathers of these women were high school graduates. A majority of women described their relationships with both their mothers and fathers as close.

At the time the baby was born, about three-fourths of the women had completed high school; by the time the child was 3 years old, four-fifths of the mothers were high school graduates. Most of the mothers had had some employment experience prior to the baby's birth. Two-thirds worked at some point or throughout the period from the baby's birth until the child's third birthday, although outside employment was most usual during the first year and a half. Most worked because they needed the money; most of the employed women liked their jobs.

The majority of women sought prenatal care in the first trimester. At all three time periods most of the women considered their health to be excellent or good. At Time 1 the majority were free of any of the six symptoms of psychiatric impairment as measured by the Langner Psychiatric Impairment Test.

When the mothers were first interviewed, almost all of the married women and a few of the unmarried women lived with male partners. By the time the children were 3 years old, about three-fourths of the mothers lived with their husbands. Most mothers considered their marital relationship to be good.

The Children

Over half of the children were male. Less than a tenth were biracial. Usually the birth was without complication. Most of the children were in good health and remained so throughout the 3-year period. As infants the children were usually described as easy to manage.

Relatively few children had experienced a disruption in the continuity of care; most remained with their mothers throughout the course of the study. The children of five unmarried mothers had been surrendered prior to the child's first birthday.

At age 3 most of the children were bowel trained, had regular sleeping habits, ate well, and were said to get along well with other children. Nearly all had begun learning table manners, how to dress and wash themselves, and brush their teeth. The majority could discriminate between some of the primary and secondary colors, knew some letters of the alphabet, could do simple counting, and were learning to draw.

Childrearing

Most of the mothers had thought about childrearing prior to the child's birth. Although most found it more difficult than they had anticipated, the majority also found it more rewarding. In fact, four-fifths of the mothers found the responsibility of child care easy. The major concern of most every mother was centered on discipline.

Supports

Most mothers had one or more close friends. The majority lived within walking or easy driving distance of their parents' home. Most had someone to turn to if they had problems regarding child care. Throughout the 3-year

172

period, the majority of mothers received some assistance with the general care of the child, usually either from the mother's parents or the child's father. At Time 3 most mothers could find someone to take over the care of the child if they wanted to go out.

Community Supports and Services

Babysitting was the need recognized by almost all the mothers; on the other hand, most said babysitters were available to them. The majority took advantage of bulletins on consumer spending. Despite the availability of several other community resources, few used them. Even among those services that were reported as available to only a limited number of women, the consensus was not particularly strong on the desirability of such services. A consistent need, expressed throughout this 3-year period, but expressed only by a fifth of the women, was a desire to meet other young mothers.

FINDINGS

Differences Between Women Married and Unmarried at Baby's Birth

Fewer of the unmarried women had been reared in intact homes; more had had changes in parental authority figures during their childhood. The fathers of the unmarried women had less education; the households in which the unmarried women were reared were larger. Not only was the relationship between the parents poorer, but the relationship of the unmarried woman to both her mother and father was less often close.

The unmarried women were younger. Fewer had completed high school; more indicated that the baby's birth had interfered with their educational aspirations. Throughout the 3-year period their income was lower; more were on welfare.

More sought employment immediately after the baby's birth. Job satisfaction was lower; more worked because they needed the money.

173

The fathers of the children were younger, less educated, and held lower level jobs. More of them were nonwhite. Their acquaintanceship with the mother had been of shorter duration. Fewer provided financial support. Fewer expressed pleasure in being a father; the baby's birth brought fewer of the couples closer.

Fewer of the unmarried women had had information about and/or access to contraceptives. More of the pregnancies had been unplanned; fewer had an early awareness that they were pregnant. More had negative reactions upon learning that they were pregnant; more considered abortion. Fewer received early prenatal care; fewer received prenatal care from a private physician. Fewer told the baby's father of the pregnancy; fewer received emotional support from the baby's father during the pregnancy period.

More of the unmarried women had felt irritable and depressed during their pregnancy; however, fewer felt fatigued. Fewer were pleased with the prospect of having a baby; more felt that it was a bad time to have a baby in view of the additional expense. More were inconsistent in their responses to feelings about being pregnant and feelings about having a baby, indicating a greater naiveté or perhaps lesser awareness of the actual consequences of an unterminated pregnancy. At the time of hospital discharge, more of the unmarried women were worried about the reactions of others to their having a baby; more were worried about finances.

Fewer of the unmarried women had given any thought to how a child should be reared; fewer used their parents as models in childrearing. During the child's infancy, more felt a loss of freedom; however, fewer expressed concern about the work entailed or about potential problems that might occur in taking care of the child. On the other hand, more were worried about how they would manage with the child's care at the time of hospital discharge.

More of the infants of the unmarried women were bottle fed. More were picked up during the night when they cried. Fewer of the children had their own bedroom; at age 3 more of them shared a bed with someone else. Fewer had their own yards in which to play.

174

The unmarried women moved more often. Fewer attended church; fewer were involved in organized group activities. Fewer were on friendly terms with their neighbors; fewer were likely to receive child care help from their neighbors.

Fewer of the unmarried women had the support of a husband or a male partner throughout the 3-year period. Although at the time their children were infants, more of the unmarried mothers anticipated help with the baby's care and more felt that they could count on more than one person in the event of an emergency, fewer of these women, in fact, received help on several specific child care tasks either then or when the children were 3 years old. Fewer received emotional support from anyone in their child care role when the children were 18 months and 3 years old.

More of the unmarried women used prenatal clinics, social agencies, baby clinics and visiting nurses. Fewer attended baby care classes. When their babies were infants, more expressed the need for financial help, infant day care, counseling, and job training. When their children were 3 years old, more unmarried women expressed interest in an adult swap shop, housing for mothers and children, and single parent groups. Fewer expressed interest in discussion groups on child care. Fewer made use of consumer spending bulletins, special instructional programs for their children and community-centered recreational facilities.

At the time their first-born child was 3, fewer of the unmarried women had given thought to family planning. Although fewer had had additional children, in those instances in which there had been further pregnancies and/or births, more of these had been unplanned.

Changes Between Time 1 and Time 3

During the 3-year period, over a tenth of the married women divorced or became separated from the father of the baby. Whereas only a very few of the unmarried women were married when they were first interviewed, about two-fifths married during the period between the baby's birth and the child's third birthday, the majority of the marriages occurring during the first 1½ years.

When first interviewed, over two-fifths of the unmarried women lived with their parents; 3 years later this was true for slightly over a tenth. Whereas slightly more than half the unmarried women were high school graduates when the babies were born, 3 years later over two-thirds had completed high school.

At Time 1, half of all the women lived within easy access of their parents' home; by Time 3 this was true for four-fifths of the women. On the other hand, frequent parental visiting had decreased to some extent. Both married and unmarried women relied less on their mothers for emotional support than they had when the children were infants; instead there was an increase in reliance upon the husband or male partner. Despite this increase, among the unmarried women emotional support in their child care role lessened in the second 1½ years; in addition, fewer of them reported that they had someone to whom they could turn should problems arise regarding the child.

The proportion of women who held outside employment increased to three-fifths during the first 1½ years; during the second year and a half it had decreased to about two-fifths. Between Time 1 and Time 3 there was a slight decrease in the proportion of married women receiving support from the child's father; among the unmarried women there was an increase--from somewhat over a third to slightly less than half. There was also a slight reduction in the number of unmarried women who received welfare.

During the second 1½ years there was a slight decrease in those who found child care easier than they had when the children were younger. Whereas at Time 2 two-thirds of the women felt that the child's presence had improved the relationship between mother and male partner, less than half the women reported this to be the case at Time 3.

Between Time 1 and Time 2 there was an increase in nearly all of the six symptoms of psychiatric impairment. Although in the case of a few of the symptoms the proportions decreased slightly, during the second year and a half the proportions reporting symptoms had become much like the proportions reporting these symptoms in the two earlier studies noted in Chapter 3.

Between Time 2 and Time 3 there was a substantial increase in those wanting group day care for their children. The numbers seeking professional help more than doubled during this same period; there was also an increase in those who now considered the possibility of seeking help as well as those who thought they might make use of their local "hot line."

During this 3-year period there was an increase in those who participated in organized group activities--from less than one-fifth of the women at Time 1 to about two-fifths at Time 3. Among the unmarried women there was an apparent increase in the recognition of the handicap of single parenting. Whereas almost two-fifths had believed this to be no handicap at Time 1, when the children were 3 years old slightly more than a fourth of the women maintained this position.

In some instances, differences between the married and unmarried women either lessened or disappeared over time. Whereas at Time 1, the median income of the married women was more than twice that of the unmarried women, by Time 3 the difference, though still substantial, was less pronounced. When interviewed shortly after the baby's birth, more unmarried women felt isolated. As their children grew older, no differences were found by marital status. At Time 2 more unmarried women believed they did not have enough money to manage; by Time 3 there were no differences in the proportions of married and unmarried women who reported this to be the case. When the children were 1½ years old, more of the unmarried than married women who lived with a husband or male partner believed their relationship had deteriorated because of the child's presence; at Time 3 there was no difference in the proportions so reporting.

More unmarried women reported "fair" or "poor" health at Time 2; at Time 3, while the proportion of women reporting health problems remained the same, there was no longer a difference between the two groups. When the children were infants the interviewers judged fewer of the unmarried women as having positive feelings toward their children; at Times 2 and 3 no differences were found between married and unmarried.

Influential Variables Affecting the Mother's Adjustment

Six measures were developed to examine the mother's adjustment and its relationhsip to the independent variables. These included the mother's contentment at Times 2 and 3, the relative ease she experienced in her child care role at these two time periods, her degree of disillusionment with the maternal role at Time 3, and a summary score that included both the Time 2 and Time 3 measures of contentment and ease in the child care role.

A total of 14 independent variables were found to be predictive of the mother's adjustment. Seven of the independent variables were associated with from two to five of the outcome measures.

Mothers who had few symptoms of psychiatric impairment were likely to have been contented, felt adequate in and accepting of their maternal role, found childrearing easy when their children were older, and scored high on the overall measure of successful outcome.

The more community resources needed but unavailable, the more likely mothers found child care difficult, were discontented with their maternal role, and scored low on the overall success measure.

Less permissive mothers were more contented, found child care easier, and scored higher on the measure of successful outcomes than did their more permissive counterparts.

Mothers who had had positive attitudes toward pregnancy found child care easier when the children were 18 months old, were more contented when the children were 3 years old and scored higher on the overall success measure than did mothers with negative or ambivalent attitudes.

The less the mothers used corporal punishment, the more likely they found child care easy and scored high on the overall measure of success.

178

The more community resources the mothers used when the children were older, the more contented the mothers and the higher the overall success score.

Mothers who scored high on the Thomas-Zander Ego Strength Scale found child care easy and were likely to be contented when their children were 18 months old.

The higher the degree of pleasure in mothering an infant, the greater the likelihood of being highly contented when the children were 18 months of age. The degree of pleasure in infant mothering was not significant in the mothers' contentment when the children were older.

Mothers living with a husband or male partner were more likely to be contented when the children were 18 months old than mothers who did not have this source of support. Whether the mothers had husbands or male partners living with them was not significant when the children were 3 years of age.

Mothers of children with several or severe health problems were more highly disillusioned with being a parent than were mothers of healthier children.

Mothers who had girls were less disillusioned with their parenting role than were mothers who had boys.

Mothers who had been under 17 years of age when they gave birth found child care more difficult when their children were 18 months old than did older mothers. The mother's age was not associated with this or any other outcome variable when the children were 3 years old.

Mothers who received a high degree of familial support during the children's early infancy were likely to find child care difficult when the children were 18 months old, as compared with mothers who had received a lesser degree of familial support. Familial support was not associated with the mothers' adjustment when the children were older.

The better the mother's physical health the more likely that she scored high on the overall measure of success.

Influential Variables Affecting the Children's Adjustment

Eight measures from the Louisville Behavior Check List were used to examine the child's adjustment at 3 years of age and its relationship to the independent variables. These included the children's scores on the following scales: aggression, inhibition, cognitive disability, normal irritability, prosocial deficit, neurotic behavior, somatic behavior, and severity level.

Seven independent variables were found to be related to the children's adjustment. With one exception, all of the independent variables were associated with three or more of the outcome measures.

The more contented mothers were more likely to have problem-free children. With the exception of the neurotic behavior scale, the degree of the mothers' contentment was associated with every measure of the children's adjustment at 3 years of age.

Children who were in the poorest health when they were 18 months old were likely to have less favorable adjustments at 3 years of age than were their healthier counterparts. The association between the child's health and adjustment was found on all but the normal irritability scale.

Children whose mothers used corporal punishment the least were most likely to be better adjusted than were children whose mothers relied on corporal punishment to a moderate or high degree. Only on the children's inhibition scores was this independent variable found not to be significant.

Boys scored better than girls on the normal irritability, neurotic behavior and inhibition scales. However, girls scored better than boys on the somatic behavior scale.

Children whose mothers had a high degree of psychiatric impairment were likely to exhibit a higher degree of symptomatology on the somatic behavior, aggression and severity level scales than were children whose mothers had fewer psychiatric symptoms.

The number of symptoms the mother reported as having experienced during pregnancy was associated with the children's cognitive disability, normal irritability, and neurotic behavior scores. The children of mothers who had reported many symptoms were most likely to be more poorly adjusted on these three outcome measures.

Children whose mothers were moderately strict were more likely to be free of disabling inhibitions than were children of mothers who were either very strict or very permissive.

IMPLICATIONS

Many of the disadvantages associated with out-of-wedlock pregnancy that had been found in earlier studies were also found in this study. These included youth, and therefore the greater likelihood of incomplete education, limited employment experience, and low income.

Despite these disadvantages, the unwed mother's decision to keep her child did not appear to be capricious. At the time the children were 3 years of age, the study was able to ascertain the whereabouts of all but 13 (7%) of the 187 children whose mothers were unmarried at the time they gave birth. One mother had died. Only five children had been surrendered for adoption. These changes had all occurred prior to the child's first birthday. In addition, three children were in foster care and two others lived with their maternal grandmothers, and in each of these instances it appeared highly unlikely that the mothers of these children would assume responsibility for their child's care. Of the 173 children whose mothers were alive and whose whereabouts were known, the vast majority (94%) were still in their mother's care.

Even if one were to assume that those 13 children who could not be located were no longer living with their mothers, it was still true that most mothers--88% of the 186 women who were still presumably alive--continued to assume responsibility for their first-born child. If these women are indeed representative of the new generation of white unwed women who choose to keep their children,* it is clear that the decision to keep their children is usually maintained, at least through the first 3 years of child care.

---

* Only three-fifths of the unwed mothers initially identified actually participated in the study. The outcomes for mother and child among participants and nonparticipants possibly might be different.

181

The fact that such a large proportion of mothers who were unmarried at the onset continued to maintain responsibility for their child's care means an increasing visibility in the community of white single parents. This, in turn, makes it easier for other pregnant unmarried women to elect to keep their child. It also may exacerbate the guilt and uncertainty of some young women who are considering adoption. In any event, it appears likely that, at least for the foreseeable future, a majority of the unmarried women who carry their babies to term will assume responsibility for the care of their children.

During the last decade or so, as more and more unmarried women have elected to keep their children and as the incidence of teen-age childbearing has increased, there has been a decreasing emphasis on the unwed mother per se and a more intensified concern for the service needs of young parents, irrespective of marital status. This study's findings support the lack of relevance of marital status to the eventual well-being of mother and child.

Although the mother's marital status at the time of her baby's birth was entered into the regression analysis of the 14 outcome variables, it was not found to be significant in contributing to the variance of any of the outcomes. It appears that despite the unmarried mother's being at least initially disadvantaged, factors other than her marital status at the time of her baby's birth may be far more important in accounting for her and her child's eventual well-being.

Contrary to expectations, the mother's age at the time of her baby's birth also proved to be relatively insignificant as a predictor of eventual outcome. However, the younger mothers in this study were not necessarily typical of today's teen-age parent. All of the women were white. They were also somewhat older than many young women who are giving birth today. Unlike many pregnant teen-agers, in the majority of instances they sought prenatal care in the first trimester, and in every instance the baby had been delivered in a hospital. The health risks were likely to be far less for these mothers and children than is the case among minority groups, younger teen-agers, mothers who do not receive early prenatal care, and those who do not use hospital medical facilities.

Community planners, in conjunction with both public and voluntary agencies, therefore, need to examine both the client characteristics and the services currently provided for parents in their communities. Is the community providing comprehensive services for young parents? Is there a substantial potential clientele that is not receiving service? Have appropriate linkages been established so that specific service needs can be met through referral?

Individual social agencies may need to reexamine their policies and practices. Agencies whose statement of purpose includes service to young mothers may have to broaden their goals in order to serve equally well those young women who keep their children as they do those who plan adoption. For those agencies committed to adoption, this may be a difficult task. If they are to expand their services to include both mothers who surrender and mothers who keep their child, they will need to engage in dialogue with agencies that have been serving the latter group. Some staff reorganization may be required, as well as provision of inservice training for both administrative and line personnel.

What do comprehensive services include? At the prevention level they include the need for young women to have far more knowledge of human sexuality, especially in the areas of conception, contraception and pregnancy. Many of the pregnancies were unplanned; most of the young mothers in the study would have preferred to have had their first child when they were older.

When they learned that they were pregnant, many of the women were unhappy. The mother's attitude toward her pregnancy was associated with three of the mothers' outcome measures; the number of symptoms she experienced during pregnancy--symptoms that may have been psychologically induced--was significant on three of the children's outcomes. This suggests the desirability of early professional intervention that would afford the opportunity for ventilation and support. Establishment of a linkage between the social agency and the "early detectors"--the private physicians, prenatal clinics, schools--could be useful in facilitating early access to the social service providers.

The well-being of the mother and her 3-year-old child was found to be closely interrelated--the more contented mother was likely to have a better adjusted child. The variable most powerful in predicting the mother's outcome was the degree of psychiatric impairment. There was a pronounced increase in psychiatric symptoms during the first 1½ years after childbirth. During the second 1½ years there was an increase in those seeking professional help as well as those considering the possibility of obtaining help. It would appear then that services should not just be directed to the pregnancy and early post-birth phase, but that, although needs may differ over time, the first 1½ years is an especially critical period during which preventive intervention programs and supportive services would be useful.

Most young mothers need support to complete their education, to have some relief from child care, to obtain vocational training, employment, and, in many instances, adequate housing. As their children grow older, the need for day care becomes evident. In addition, many young mothers need the opportunity to interact with others who are in the same situation.

These and other resources, not available to some mothers in this study, were found to be crucial to the mothers' well-being. In addition to the degree of the mother's psychiatric impairment, the one other variable significantly related to five of the six outcome measures of the mothers was the number of needed but unavailable community resources. The fewer the number of needed, but unavailable community resources, the more likely that at both Time 2 and Time 3 the mother found child care easier and was more contented, and the more likely that she also scored high on the overall success measure.

On the other hand, we found that most mothers had knowledge about and access to community services, should they choose to use them. The fact that so few of these young women availed themselves of community services may have reflected a lack of motivation, but also may be a reflection of weaknesses in service content and service delivery. Do the services have a flexibility and capability to attract and assist mothers with varying degrees of education and sophistication? How much do the professionals reach out to and, in effect, initially bring new mothers into testing for themselves the value of available services?

Childrearing is not easy. The new mother does not set out with the intention of rearing her child poorly. Many mothers in the study simply gave childrearing and child care little thought. They took their parenting role for granted, with little or no reflection on their own needs or those of the children they were bringing into the world. Traditional social agency services and child development courses were not being used by most of the women, doubtless because of a lack of motivation or felt need, and perhaps also because they were believed to be too formally structured.

However, many mothers admitted that they felt isolated, and the proportions expressing this feeling increased during the first 1½ years. The profusion of self-help groups, from Alcoholics Anonymous to the more recent Parents Anonymous, suggest the value of the informal peer group as a means of involvement as well as a means of assisting in problem solving. The fact that at all three interviews a substantial proportion of women expressed a desire to meet with other new mothers may be not only an expression of the isolation experienced by many of the women but an indication of their interest and willingness to engage in peer group learning and support. Mothers' groups, with minimal professional leadership and guidance that facilitate rather than direct the content and direction of discussion, could be established in neighborhood schools, churches, community centers or other public or semipublic places in which space is available.

Such groups would provide opportunity to enrich the mother's social life, as well as giving her the needed encouragement and support in her child care role. Informal mothers groups contain remedial aspects as well. Disci-

185

pline was found to be a matter of concern for many of the mothers in this study. The degree of permissiveness and the use of corporal punishment were also associated with outcome for mother and child. Group discussion of effective but not potentially harmful methods of discipline, as well as the imposition of constructive limitations on behavior, two aspects of childrearing that were found significantly related to several of the outcome variables, may well be welcomed by and beneficial to new mothers. The very act of sharing experiences with others who may have had or are currently having similar problems provides continual relief as well as digestible education.

Many of us no longer believe that every woman has the "natural" capacity for mothering. The heavy sales of books on infant and child care are certainly an indication of the parental need to know more. The young new mother is frequently alone for many hours of the day with her child. If she is unemployed, frequently she has minimal peer companionship. If she is employed, as was the case for many of these young women, usually she still must assume responsibility for her child's care when she returns home. In either event the young mother is faced with the responsibility for the life of another human being. Community supports and services are crucial. The community must see that services are geared to the needs of their particular population, and that these services are in fact accessible to the various types of young parents in their community.